DAPPING

The Exciting Way of Fishing Flies
that Fly, Quiver, and Jump

Robert H. Boyle

Photographs by Kathryn Belous-Boyle

STACKPOLE
BOOKS

To Andy Minnig and Lynn Marsh and all the advocates for Cherry Valley

Copyright © 2007 by Robert H. Boyle

Published by
STACKPOLE BOOKS
5067 Ritter Road
Mechanicsburg, PA 17055
www.stackpolebooks.com

Printed in China

First edition

10 9 8 7 6 5 4 3 2 1

Library of Congress Cataloging-in-Publication Data

Boyle, Robert H.
  Dapping : guide to the traditional method for fishing flies that fly, quiver, and jump / by Robert H. Boyle ; photographs by Kathryn Belous-Boyle. — 1st ed.
      p. cm.
  Includes bibliographical references and index.
  ISBN-13: 978-0-8117-0142-6 (hardcover)
  ISBN-10: 0-8117-0142-5 (hardcover)
  1. Dapping (Fishing) I. Title.

SH456.12.B69 2007
799.12'4—dc22
                                                    2006019057

CONTENTS

. . . dapping my griffeen, burning water in the spearlight or catching trophies of the king's royal college of sturgeone by the armful to bake pike . . .

—James Joyce, *Finnegans Wake*

You stick them on the hook without any shot and just flick them to and fro on the surface—"dapping" they call it.

—George Orwell, *Coming Up for Air*

PREFACE

THE ONLY ONE OF ITS KIND, THIS BOOK IS DEVOTED TO DAPPING, a way of fly fishing new to Americans. Dapping ranges from the ancient method of simply touching the fly up and down—dap-dap-dap—on the surface of the water, to the modern (well, since the early nineteenth century) use of blowline, introduced to me by Jon Shaw, by which the wind carries the fly to fish that see neither leader nor line, only a dish to be devoured.

While all the flies described here are primarily designed for dapping, they also offer new ideas and approaches for tying materials, tools, procedures, and tactics to both the fly tier and the dedicated fly caster.

Parts of chapter 3, "My Primitive Dapping," first appeared in *Sports Illustrated*, May 29, 1989, and *Outdoor Life*, September 1996; part of chapter 7, "Disrespected Crane Flies," first appeared in *Fly Fisherman*, February 2002; and part of chapter 8, "Jumping Grass Shrimp," first appeared in *Field and Stream*, June 1998. I have added to those last two chapters because information about grass shrimp and crane flies is lacking in the fly-fishing literature. (In contrast, given the wealth of literature on mayflies and caddis, there are no chapters per se about those insects, but it does not take much to imagine the lively role that dapping can play in imitating the antics of the adults.)

Present and past thanks to Judith Schnell, Amy Lerner, Jon Shaw, Howard Bartholomew, Bob Mead, Dick Dahlgren, Harry Smith, Bob Brown, Bill Catherwood, Charlie (Faithful Correspondent) Lewis, David Beazley, S. A. Neff Jr., Alex Zagoreos, Ken Callahan, Judith Bowman, Jose Manual Cenador Cela, Nick Rae, and Peter Dunne;

Jack Hoffinger, Phyllis Dunning, Andy and Kathy Minnig, and Paul Solomon for generously allowing me use of their lakes and ponds; J. P. Ross, Ted Niemeyer, Eric Leiser, Pete and Jan Zito, Cliff Schwark, Paul Schmookler, Anthony Henry Smith (just for listening), John Betts (the first to tell me about blowlining), the late Jack Olsen and the late Harry Darbee, Katherine ("Is it finished?") Sweeney, Ralph Graves (for reasons he may not remember because he is so giving), and finally to the one and only Guy Danella for his boundless good humor, technological expertise, and generosity of time.

Thanks also to Paul Morgan, publisher of Coch-y-Bonddu Books, for permission to quote from *Angling: The Solitary Vice* by Fred Buller; Mick Lunn, for permission to quote from *A Particular Lunn: One Hundred Glorious Years on the Test* by Mick Lunn and Clive Graham-Ranger; Philip Monahan, editor of *American Angler*, for permission to quote from the May/June 1998 article by Charles Gaines; and the University of Southern California, on behalf of the Hancock Foundation Archive, for permission to reproduce the drawings illustrating the differences between grass shrimps from *A General Revision of the Palaemonidae (Crustacea decapoda natantia) of the Americas* by Lipke B. Holthuis.

CHAPTER ONE

Dapping
is a Breeze

Sacred cows make the tastiest hamburger.
—Abbie Hoffman

APPING IS THE MOST EXCITING WAY OF FLY FISHING. IT IS ALSO the easiest way: literally a breeze in its advanced form with blowline, because the wind, even a puff, carries the fly to the fish. Though popular in Ireland and Scotland, few Americans know anything about it, yet it saves the day when casting is impossible.

With the wind from behind, the fly fisher equipped with a dapping rod and blowline can seemingly conjure up fish like a magician with a wand. It is entirely different from casting, as if you could win at golf just by putting the ball in the hole with your hand while everyone else had to keep using clubs.

You need a long rod for dapping. The rod I use is the Shakespeare Dapper 1302-520. Oddly enough, even though Shakespeare is an American company based in Columbia, South Carolina, it does not sell the rod in the United States, and I had to get mine from England.

Besides Shakespeare, dealers in old tackle occasionally offer antique dapping rods at rather high prices to collectors, while an Irish firm, Turas Fly Rods, in Dublin, sells The Grand Dapper, a highly crafted 17-foot, five-piece rod for €866, or about $1,100. In contrast, my Shakespeare Dapper, which is also 17 feet long, cost only

1

$75. It comes in five sections and handily telescopes down to a mere four feet two inches. I rig it with a three-foot leader of 6- to 10-pound test with one of the dapping flies set forth in this book.

The short leader is attached to a length of blowline, a special ultralight floss also known as sail because it catches the wind like the sail on a boat. I knot it every foot to keep the floss from fraying, and depending on the strength of the wind and how far I want the fly to reach, the length of the blowline usually runs between four and eight feet and on occasion much longer. Put in sailing terms, in a light breeze, put on more sail; in a heavy wind, take in more sail.

The backing attached to the blowline is monofilament of 10-pound test or more, depending on the quarry sought, and anathema to fly-rod purists, I dispense with the sacred fly reel and its consecrated fly line. Instead I put the backing on a sacrilegious spinning reel. I care not if the purists catch me *flagrante delicto*. I could also use a bait-casting reel or, as many do in Ireland and Scotland, a center-pin reel.

Why no fly reel with fly line? A couple of reasons: First of all, fly line is not only unnecessary, it is an impediment, literally a drawback, because it is much heavier than mono, and, in obedience to the law of gravity, fly line on a long, upright dapping rod will slide back down through the guides, pulling the blowline with it. Second, the retrieve on a fly reel is far too slow for dapping. You need a reel with a fast retrieve to bring in a fish and keep the blowline from getting wet. In addition, if the wind radically shifts direction, you need a fast retrieve to prevent the fly and the blowline from hanging up in a tree or risk having the fly blown back in your face.

All together, my dapping rod and fully loaded reel weigh a shade over two pounds. The weight doesn't bother me if I'm catching fish, but on a long day of dapping it can be tiring. To avoid that on a boat, rest the butt on the deck between your legs, and for dapping on land, place the butt in a stripping basket or buy a carpenter's belt from a hardware store and rest the butt in the middle pocket.

To fish, the dapper simply raises the rod upright and uses the wind from behind to carry the blowline, leader, and fly over the

Ready the dapping rod at waterside so that you don't hang it up in trees or brush. Instead of a fly reel, use a spinning or bait-casting reel for a quick retrieve.

With the wind at your back, let the blowline carry the fly.

water. The fly is carried by the wind, and in response to the dapper's movements of the rod, gently alights, sits with feathers and fibers twitching, tantalizingly dances and prances across the surface, and if no strike results, takes to the air where it seductively hovers before landing again to start the cycle anew, its antics exactly like that of a living creature doing what comes naturally. This successful replication of nature is not only the essence of fly fishing, it also exposes the fallacy of Frederic M. Halford's dead-drift dogma that has shackled dry-fly fishing for more than a century.

No fly caster, no matter how gifted, can make a fly put on such a performance. Irresistible to fish, it can drive salmon, trout, bass, panfish, and a yet-to-be-counted number of saltwater species crazy with desire. The same goes for the dapper. "One watches the fly quivering on the water with the tense expectancy that one watches a float, and the thrill of the rise is heart-stopping: usually every stage of the take can be seen," wrote the great Hugh Falkus in *Salmon Fishing*.

The strike can come at any time, even when the fly is airborne. Want to see a fish get a hernia? Go dapping. Bluegills with the potbelly of a Chicago alderman will heavily hurl themselves from the water, and I recently read about a sea trout that rocketed three feet out of a Scottish loch for a dapped fly.

For the rankest novice, ten to fifteen minutes of practicing with a dapping rod and blowline should be enough to begin fishing. To quote Falkus again: "This ease of fishing makes dapping an ideal method for wives and camp followers, who know little about angling but fancy having a try themselves."

For the novice, the one difficulty might come in setting the hook. Set the hook when the fish strikes, and the fish escapes. Despite the instinct to set the hook, you must wait for the fish to turn down with the fly. Time yourself before setting the hook by whispering "one, two, three," or exclaiming, as Brits do, "God save the Queen!" Or you may want to shout, "God bless America!" Say whatever you wish, but then set the hook hard by striking upward with a quick stroke of your whole arm. Or you may want to say nothing and do as Scottish ghillies advise: get blind drunk so your reaction is slowed and the fish hooks itself.

Dapping has a reputation for attracting big fish, and for the veteran fly fisher searching for that legendary monster brown, dapping is ideal: no worry about fussing around for the finest and longest leader or splattering a cast that could spook the fish, and of course, no drag or line to mend. Absolutely nothing touches the water, not even a shadow, except your fly strutting its stuff, the ultimate imitation of nature.

This is not to say that fish are guaranteed. They never are, but a dapping rod and blowline give the fly fisher an edge on a breezy day and are definitely a boon on days too windy for casting. An axiom of fly casting says that the wind blows at least 80 percent of the time. Indeed, it is a rare day when it doesn't reach at least 5 miles per hour, which is considered a light breeze on the Beaufort Wind Scale, yet it is sufficient to rustle leaves, turn weather vanes—and make a dapped fly airborne. A moderate breeze on the Beaufort scale, one with a force of 13 to 18 mph (enough to raise dust and loose paper) can interfere with fly casting. A fresh breeze of 19 to 24 mph, one which sways small trees in leaf and forms crested wavelets on inland waters, can cause a caster to turn in for the day. But this doesn't faze the dapper, not even in wind-swept Patagonia. It's glory time.

Take this incident that occurred one August evening on the South Fork of the Snake River in Idaho, the sun about a half hour from setting. A fresh breeze of 20 mph chased fly rodders off the river and into the bar of Mark Rockefeller's South Fork Lodge. As they sip their drinks they see, to their surprise, a bearded man, obviously a guest new to the lodge, determinedly striding across the lawn down to the river with an extraordinarily long rod. "Don't get hit by lightning!" shouts a would-be wit, followed by hoots and laughter from the rest of the bar crowd.

Unbeknownst to the bar crowd, the man is a dapper. He raises the rod straight up with his right hand and holds it there. The joshing, noisy bar crowd is too far away to see the fly, a grasshopper imitation, but some manage to spot what looks like an unusually thick line billowing upstream. And soon they see a bend in the rod followed by a fish vaulting from the water. "I was praying that a fish would take it straight away to quiet them," the dapper recalls. His prayers answered, he returns a 12-inch rainbow to the river, and the bar crowd, now quiet, abandoning chairs and spilling drinks, scurries down to the river to watch. By the time darkness falls and the dapper releases the last of half a dozen rainbows and browns, he is besieged with questions, all admiring even if slurred.

The next day, the wind is even stronger, straight out upriver, as the dapper hikes to a shingled island. Conditions are ideal for him.

Be prepared to reel in quickly and move if the wind shifts toward you.

No one else is fishing because casting a fly would be impossible. He wades in, the blowline sails out, the fly lands, and he begins taking fish. Drift boats go downriver with glum guides and glummer fly rodders. Two guides with boats and four sports aboard pull up on the opposite shore to eat an early lunch—what else is there to do?—and watch the man release fish after fish after fish. Later that day, the two guides and the four sports come by the lodge to render homage and ask just what was he doing and how was he doing it with that weird rod and line. He gladly tells them and gives them lengths of blowline to try for themselves.

The dapper was Jonathan Shaw, my blowline mentor, an Englishman so eager to spread the dapping gospel to anyone who will listen that I call him Jon the Daptist. Jon is a wildlife artist who lives in Maryland on the eastern shore of the Chesapeake Bay with

Anne, his American wife. Although a skilled fly caster who has "killed," as the Brits say, three hundred Atlantic salmon, he is smitten with dapping, which he took up in 1980 on Loch Maree in Scotland, because there is no other way to make an artificial fly cavort like its natural counterpart.

In 1997, three years after we met, I told Andrew Revkin, a fly fisher and reporter for *The New York Times* who lived nearby, about Jon, and Andy wound up writing a lengthy feature about Jon dapping in the East Branch of the Croton River. This led to Jon speaking at the Catskill Fly Fishing Center and the formation of the Royal American Dapping Club.

Andy's article also prompted *American Angler* magazine to ask British writer Charles Gaines to write a piece on dapping. It appeared in the May/June 1998 issue, in which Gaines wrote, "Does dapping have any sort of viability in the U. S.? I believe it has: certainly on your lakes and ponds, but equally in the faster sections of rivers like the Henrys Fork, certainly in such big rivers as the Madison, the South Fork, the Yellowstone, and so on. In fact, dapping will work anywhere trout demand delicate presentation, anywhere where trout have seen just about every other fly-fishing trick and technique. Apart from all that, it's fun, which is, after all, why we fish."

CHAPTER TWO

The Evolution
of Dapping

DESPITE THE MISTY HISTORY SURROUNDING THE ORIGINS OF dapping, it probably began at least two thousand years ago with bait, live or dead, or a lure. Homer mentions use of rod and line, and centuries later, around 200 AD, Aelian, a Roman, wrote the first known account of fishing with artificial flies. In his *Natural History*, he described Macedonians who tied flies of red wool and two cock feathers around a hook to catch "fish with speckled skins" in a river called the Astreus: "Their rod is six feet long, and their line is the same length. Then they throw their snare, and the fish, attracted and maddened by the colour, comes straight at it, thinking from the pretty sight to gain a dainty mouthful; when, however, it opens its jaw, it is caught by the hook, and enjoys a bitter repast, a captive."

Artificial flies were described in *The Treatyse of Fysshnge wyth an Angle*, published in 1496 and attributed to Dame Juliana Berners, an English nun whose authorship, and even her very existence, has been questioned. Fishing with stout wooden rods and horsehair line, anglers of the dame's era could not cast any distance, so they had to dunk their bait or dap live insects or artificial flies on the surface of the water.

In 1613, in *Secrets of Angling*, John Dennys called dapping "bushing" because the angler hid behind a bush while touching a fly on the surface. (Dapping from behind bushes and trees was also called "shade-fishing"; the ultimate shade fisher was Birch, an Oxford don, who lived up to his name by dressing as a tree.) Later that century Izaak Walton advised in *The Compleat Angler*, "Let no part of your line touch the water, but your fly only, and still be moving your fly upon the water." Rods 15 to 18 feet long were the order of the day, and in his addition to the fifth edition of Walton's book, Charles Cotton wrote that the dapper should use "a short line, not much more than half the length of your rod, if you have any wind to carry it from you. And this way of fishing we call Daping, Dabbing, or Dibbing. Wherein you are always to have your line flying before you, up or down river as the wind serves, and to angle as near to you as you can to the bank of the same side whereon you stand, though where you see a fish near, you may guide your fly quick over him, whether in the middle or on the contrary side; and if you are pretty well out of sight, either by kneeling, or the interposition of a bank or bush, you may be almost sure to raise and take him too, if it be presently done." One very windy evening, Cotton caught thirty-five "great trout" by dapping with live Green Drake mayflies.

In the early nineteenth century, according to *Angling: The Solitary Vice*, by Fred Buller, a recent scholarly work published by Coch-y-Bonddu Books in Wales, dapping got a "tremendous boost" with "the development of the silk-floss line and its subsequent appearance in the tackle shops during the nineteenth century." The precise date is not known, but "the availability of the multi-stranded silk-floss line (dubbed the blow-line because even a light breeze would carry it out, plus fly and leader, as far as the fisherman required) brought a new perspective to dapping for river trout when used in conjunction with a fishing reel. The method has survived to this day as a superlative means of catching brown trout or sea trout from Scottish lochs or Irish loughs with either natural or artificial flies."

Although dapping with blowline flowered in nineteenth-century England, it was surprisingly unknown to the very influential W. C. Stewart, the cocksure Scot who advocated fishing upstream in his widely read book *The Practical Angler,* which was first published in 1857 and in which he declared: "No method of angling can imitate the hovering flight of an insect along the surface of the water, now just touching it, then flying a short distance, and so on; and for the angler to attempt any motion of his hand to give his flies a living appearance is mere absurdity."

Dapping also had its adversaries, notably the doubly named Francis Francis, from 1856 to 1893 the plump, bearded angling editor of *The Field,* the sporting bible of the Victorian age in Britain. Francis was known to fish for barbel with a worm, yet when his landmark work, *A Book on Angling,* first appeared in 1867, he condemned "dibbing" or "daping" as "hardly fair fishing; indeed, dibbing, more especially with the May fly, is so destructive when worked by an adept, that it is more than a question of whether it should be held fair fishing at all."

However, having said that, Francis, obviously not wanting to lose out on potential sales of his book, then went on to state that inasmuch "as many clubs and good anglers do follow and profess it, and as in many lakes it yields almost the only sport got from them, I will e'en treat of it."

Dapping called for a 19- to 20-foot rod "and often beyond that," Francis wrote. The rod "generally resembles the mast of a fishing-smack, being of the lightest cane, but as long as it can be obtained or worked." The dapper used blowline to carry an impaled mayfly, sometimes two of them, or an artificial fly, to the fish, with the blowline "the lightest, loosest, and airiest floss silk—so weblike that the least puff of wind will drive before it. Light and loose as it is, it has abundant strength. . . . The angler then chooses that bank of the stream whence the wind is blowing, and walks up the bank; when he sees a good fish rise, he turns his back to the wind, faces the fish, lets out line enough just to clear the ground—holds the rod perfectly upright, and allows the wind to take the line out over the river, which, if but a very moderate breeze is on, it will do easily. When it is bellied out half-way or three-parts across the stream, judging his distance carefully, the angler slowly lowers the point of the rod, so that if he has measured his distance pretty rightly the fly will light where or whereabouts the fish is rising, and a little above it of course, and as the fly can be lowered on to the water au naturel like thistledown, and by the skillful working of the rod-point can even be made to skip and flutter up and down on the surface like the natural insect in the enjoyment of the most rabid and demonstrative liberty, and as no line need be visible, and nothing need touch the water but the fly."

Despite his condemnation of dapping with live insects, "especially with the May fly," in near breathless prose, Francis went on to advise, or should one say confide: "There are many other natural flies that can be used in daping, as the stone fly, the alder fly, the blue-bottle, the daddy long legs, the coch-y-bondu, the cinnamon, etc., in fact almost any fly that is large enough to be stuck upon a hook will answer the purpose. For the smaller flies it is customary to use a smaller hook, and to put two flies upon it; but with such flies it is more customary . . . to dib in over bushes or from behind some sheltering tree, or any other cover where the angler can conceal himself. Here, haply, where overhanging branches cast a shadow on the water in the hottest weather, the big fellows lie close in to the bank under which

    . . . beneath the tangled roots
    Of pendent trees, the monarch of the brook

has his abiding-place: you see him, as it were standing at his front door in the recipt of custom, and rising gently at every fly, grub or insect-security that may pass him. It is your business, oh angler! to take in this greedy discounter of insect acceptances."

Three years later in London the grandly named Delabere P. Blaine, Esq., produced *An Encyclopedia of Rural Sports*, in which he advised: "With a strong wind, the angler should keep his rod steady in one position, taking the wind rather slantingly behind, and allowing the breeze itself to carry the line, he should watch a momentary lull in the gale, when by lowering his hand he may drop the fly on the surface as gently and naturally as possible."

It is worth noting that when the Houghton Club on the River Test, for the past hundred years the revered bastion of casting the dry fly, began in 1822, blowlining was the way to fish. In John Waller Hills' *River Keeper*, his 1936 biography of William James Lunn, he wrote that in 1887 when Lunn assumed the post of keeper at the Houghton Club, "members sometimes fished with the artificial in the grannom [caddis] season, but for the mayfly they used nothing but the natural fly on a blow-line, except at night, or when there was no wind blowing. Even with the grannom the blow-line was still common, and in the mayfly season it was almost universal. The rod was eighteen to twenty feet long, usually of bamboo, the line undressed silk [floss], with a gut casting line [leader] of three yards. With this a good blower could get out thirty or forty yards of line, working it out gradually, and, of course, keeping the fly and the line off the water all the time."

Lunn's grandson, Mick, the third in the family to become the Houghton Club keeper, collaborated with Clive Graham-Ranger in writing *A Particular Lunn: One Hundred Glorious Years on the Test*, published in 1990. In it, Mick Lunn noted that when his grandfather took over "fly fishers could be roughly divided into two categories: the blowers, who used the blowline and a natural fly; and the whippers, who used the [greenheart] whipping rod and the artificial wet fly. . . .

"Once the blowline was ready the ghillies netted a box of grannom, mayflies or caperers (which are summer sedges), depending on the time of year, and impaled the mature insect on the hook: two grannom flies were recommended, but only one mayfly or caperer. The member would then work out 30-40 yards of line in the wind, making sure not to let the line or the fly touch the water until the fly was blown over a rising fish, at which moment it was guided expertly onto the water. . . .

"The change to upstream fishing with a single fly to a specific rising trout was largely brought about in the late 1800s and early 1900s by the writings of Frederic Halford. He insisted that for any flyfisher to succeed, he had to have a box of tiny artificials, each tied to closely imitate the natural flies the trout were feeding on. Halford and his many avid followers were purists and they laid down the basic rules of dry fly fishing, which have survived on our chalkstreams to this day."

The year 1904 marked the last of blowlining at the Houghton Club and probably elsewhere in England around that time. "But why did blow-lining—that superlative method of catching river trout—die out?" Buller asks. "I think there are two reasons. First of all it is likely that the technical progress of fly-line making [especially following the introduction of braided, tapered, oiled silk lines from America in the 1870s] and rod making allowed fishermen to fish from both banks of a river at all times whereas it was only possible to fish the blow-line when the wind allowed and then only downwind.

"Secondly, an elitism probably developed after it was seen that the accomplished few, using the new double-tapered lines with short rods that were powerful enough to push them into the wind, were able to display enviable skills."

Certainly this must mark one of the few times in history in which the boast, "My rod is shorter than your rod," made one angler more macho than another.

Interestingly, just as dapping was dying out in England, it apparently led A. H. E. Wood to come up with the idea for a new method of fishing for salmon. It came to him on an Irish river on a hot July day in 1903 after the salmon ignored all his flies. Tired of casting, Wood gave up and went to the head of the pool, which was bounded by an eel weir. There he found, as he described in *Salmon Fishing*, edited by Eric Taverner, "a number of salmon with their noses pushed right up to the end of the sill. As luck had it, I happened to have with me a White Moth trout fly; this I tied on the end of the cast and sat on the plank-bridge over the weir. Then holding the gut in my hand, I dibbed the fly over them. After some minutes, one of the salmon became curious enough to rise up to examine the fly, but at the last moment thought better of it; this I believe was due to its attention having been distracted by my feet, which were dangling over the plank, barely six feet away from the water. I changed my position, knelt on the bridge and let down the fly. This time the fish came more boldly at the fly, and it was followed by others; but I had pricked several before I realized that, because I was kneeling directly above them, I was, in striking, pulling the hook straight out of their mouths. So I changed my tactics, and by letting go the cast at the right moment, succeeded in dropping the fly actually into the open mouth of the next fish that came up to it. I then picked up my rod, ran off the bridge, and made all haste downstream. All this time the line and cast were slack and floating down; yet when I tightened on the fish, I found it had hooked itself. By the use of this trick I landed six fish, lost others, and pricked more than I care to say, all in a few hours. After that experience, I discovered myself fishing on the surface or as near to it as I was able. The final advance came, when I started using a greased line to assist in keeping the fly in the right position, and I thus evolved out of a simple experiment what has become a most interesting mode of salmon-angling, the greased line method."

And speaking of Ireland, what about dapping there? Its beginning as dibbing is lost in time, but the large, shallow wind-blown lakes with their mayfly hatches were natural incubators for its development, and from there the practice of blowlining apparently jumped across the Irish Sea to Scotland seventy or so years ago. According to W. A. Adamson's 1960 book, *Lake and Loch Fishing for Salmon and Sea Trout*: ". . . the origin of its present vogue in Scotland is usually ascribed to a Mr. Ainger. At Loch Maree in the 1930's, he decided to try out the Irish method using an artificial fly (a Loch Ordie, perhaps) and he had considerable success." Other dappers followed.

Now is just the time for Americans to do the same.

CHAPTER THREE

My Primitive Dapping

I KNEW VERY LITTLE ABOUT ITS EVOLUTION WHEN I FIRST BEGAN dapping, or what I took to be dapping, in a very roundabout, primitive way in April of 1988. I had no idea that in the course of the next six years I would be repeating two thousand years of history—a vivid example of angling phylogeny recapitulating ontogeny—but my efforts were not without success, and I recount them here because they may be of benefit to the reader.

The lake next to our place outside Cold Spring had largemouths, but the bass season in New York didn't open until late June, and so I decided to catch some bluegills for dinner. I wanted them to be at least seven inches long so I could conveniently fillet them.

I could easily see bluegills of assorted sizes swimming just below the surface about ten to twenty feet from the dam, but whenever I cast a fly from the dam one of the horde of smaller fish would dart over and take it. As I watched the bigger bluegills cruise around unscathed, a phone company jingle popped into my mind: "Reach out and touch someone."

I knew just the lure that would take them: a $\frac{1}{64}$-ounce fly-rod jig of my own devising on a size 10 to 14 hook. I first tied it back in the late 1960s, well before the Clouser Minnow appeared on the scene, to catch alewives coming in from the Atlantic to spawn in the lower Croton River, a tributary of the Hudson. Later I named it the Kat's Meow after Dmitri "Mitya" Kotyik, one of my wife's two Siamese cats. (A full description of the Kat's Meow and its usefulness in dapping with blowline appears in chapter 9.)

What I needed now was a long rod to reach out with the Kat's Meow for the bigger bluegills. I went to Richie and Pat Ferris's Croton Bait & Tackle Shop, a mom and pop basement operation where all sorts of wonderful odd stuff was to be found, and bought a 12-foot cane pole for $3. On my return home I attached six feet of 4-pound-test monofilament to the tip, tied on a Kat's Meow, and hustled to the lake. Reaching out over the water, I could target a big bluegill and dap the jig on the surface within an inch or two of the target's nose. In about half an hour I caught fifteen bluegills that met or exceeded my 7-inch minimum.

That summer I took my second step toward dapping after hearing about the French way of fishing on Esopus Creek in the Catskill Mountains. Different parts of the Catskills have long served as vacation ground for ethnic groups from New York City, with enclaves of Ukranians, Armenians, Irish, Jews, Poles, Hungarians, Germans, Latin Americans, and French pocketed here and there. The French focus on the Esopus Valley, where many fish for browns and the big wild rainbows that run down the creek to fatten themselves on herring, also known as sawbellies, in the Ashokan Reservoir, a sort of miniature inland version of the ocean, before running back up the creek when it's time to spawn.

Most Catskill fly fishermen I knew scorned the French fishermen because they didn't fish with fly rods. Instead they dapped with very long and strange rods that allowed them to take trout unaware that anyone was after them. I did not dismiss the French out of hand, though; I was intrigued and believed that they would have something to teach me.

In France, indeed in all of Europe, including Great Britain and Ireland, anglers lack the great variety and abundance of fishing opportunities that we take for granted in the United States, so they must innovate. We may laugh at news pictures of dozens of Alfies and Berties in their flat caps lined up along a dismal Midlands canal, the rain pouring down, sitting in folding chairs under their "brollies," holding a death-grip on 30- or 40-foot-long rods in a match competition for what we would dismiss as minnows, teensy-weensy fish that they store in a keep net for the prize-money weigh-in, after which they return the fishies to the canal. But the very fact that they're using such extraordinarily long rods, or "poles" as they call them, hints at something: They know what they're doing because they're forced to develop such sophisticated tackle and techniques.

Take carp, please—as Henny Youngman might say. To Americans carp are trash fish, but across the Atlantic the Brits in particular absolutely venerate them. Big carp are stars, big draws in a competitive day-ticket fishing industry in which you must pay to fish. In England or France or any place in Europe, if you should shoot one with a bow and arrow or rifle, as some here do, you'd be crucified (which may explain the existence of crucian carp).

In Britain, three times as much money is spent on fishing for carp and coarse fish as on trout and salmon, and I hazard that the same holds true on the Continent. Europeans buy specialized baits; radio-controlled model boats that carry the bait and unload it far from shore; electronic bite alarms that ring in case any one of them is snoring in a bed chair; all this stuff and more sold by tackle stores.

To lure these couch potatoes to day-ticket water to fish from a peg, an assigned spot that is their allotted space between the other potatoes, the proprietor of a carp lake will pay as much as $5,000 for a 30-pounder to attract clientele. And this big 'un will be given a name. Catch him or her, and in Britain you'll get your picture taken for the tabloid *Angling Times* before you lovingly return extra-large Penelope or Percy to the water unharmed. Humongous carp with names that resonate throughout carpdom, like NFL quarterbacks or home-run hitters here, have been caught so often that they become very hard to catch because they've smartened up and know how to feel the hook inside the bait and turn away from temptation. An acquaintance of Jon the Daptist astounded all England when he began catching one famous uncatchable big 'un after another with ease. His secret? He would secure the bait, no hook inside, on the end of a hair-thin line, the hook an inch above the bait. Sagacious Penelope or Percy would mouth the bait with no hook, suck it in, and—presto, gotcha!

In Europe then, with its multitude of cheek-by-jowl, shoulder-to-shoulder countries, ideas and techniques flow readily across fishing frontiers, as witness the 40-foot poles, radio-controlled boats, and electronic bite alarms, to say nothing of the flying condoms for salmon and the Czech nymph for trout. Which is why I wanted to meet the French on the Esopus.

I phoned a man I've known for almost forty years, Larry Solomon, coauthor with Eric Leiser of *The Caddis and the Angler* and a member of the Theodore Gordon Fly Fishers, and he suggested that I get in touch with Larry Kovi, who grew up spending his summers in the Hungarian enclave upstream of the French enclave. Until Kovi was in his late teens he fished Esopus Creek the French way. He filled me in on the French and suggested that I visit the L'Auberge des Quatre Saisons, French for "the Inn of the Four Seasons," in Shandaken.

In the early 1950s Edouard LaBeille, a former Paris fireman who was working as a waiter at Le Pavillon, the first great postwar French restaurant in Manhattan, started vacationing in the Esopus Valley. LaBeille was a fisherman and hunter, and in 1954 he bought an old boardinghouse in Shandaken, fixed it up, added a restaurant, and named the place L'Auberge des Quatre Saisons. As word of the Auberge spread down in the city, it made the valley popular with French diplomats, airline pilots, hairdressers, restaurant owners, and others homesick for countryside like Ariege or le Pays Basque. The

You never can tell when a fish may hit, but when it does, pause and say, "God bless America." Then set the hook by vigorously striking up with your entire arm.

trout fishing in the Esopus was a major draw, too, because the creek was rated one of the most productive trout streams in the East.

On a Saturday night in July, my wife and I drove up to the Auberge for dinner, and there, it turned out, I discovered that the thirty-six-year-old maitre d', Emile Melin, a slim, sandy-haired man with a boyish smile, was known as the best French trout fisherman on the Esopus. Alas, Emile did not use flies. "I am zee specialeest in werhhhms," he said. Nevertheless, I was interested in knowing how well he did, and after I asked, he bustled off to the kitchen and returned with a tray containing two rainbow trout frozen in a block of ice. "Voila," he said. One weighed three pounds, the other two.

Emile said that he started fishing as a boy in Vichy. When he was twenty-nine he came to Manhattan, took a job as a maitre d', began fishing Esopus Creek on his days off, and eventually wound up working year-round at the Auberge so he could fish and hunt. Emile readily agreed to let me watch him fish Esopus Creek for trout, and two days later at 9 A.M. I returned to the inn. He put his gear in the trunk of my car and directed me to a bait shop where he bought worms. Back in the car, we drove west along Route 28 bordering the Esopus and parked next to the bridge leading to Woodland Valley.

The sun was already blistering hot, not a cloud overhead, in short not an ideal day at all to fish, but no matter to Emile, who put on hip boots and took out what appeared to be a 2-foot fiberglass rod. Pulling on one end, he kept untelescoping the rod until it reached its full length of 15 feet. It had no guides, but he attached a tiny reel no bigger than a silver dollar to the butt. The reel, he said, held about 35 feet of 10-pound-test monofilament line. I had never seen anything like it and asked, "What happens when a fish runs?"

"Zey don't run anywhere," he said.

"But where are the guides?" I asked.

Emile said that the 10-pound-test line went through a ceramic tunnel inside the rod. He took a weighted needle, attached the line to it, inserted the needle into the hollow butt end, and standing on the bridge, pointed the rod tip down toward the creek and let gravity slide the needle with line down through the rod.

Next Emile pinched two split-shot on a snelled 6-inch leader with a size 8 bait hook. He explained that the long rod without guides allowed him to put the worm wherever he wanted within a 20-foot radius without hanging up or frightening the fish.

He climbed down to the creek and threaded a worm on the hook. Holding the rod in his right hand and fingering the line near the reel in his left, he gently swung the rod upstream, and the worm landed twenty feet away in a strong flow of water. As the flow carried the bottom-bouncing worm downstream, Emile followed it with the rod held straight out at arm's length. He did this five times. Nothing.

He shuffled a couple of feet out into the creek, climbed up on a rock, and swung the worm downstream into a pocket behind another rock. A trout struck. He swung the fish toward him, rapped the 10-inch brown on the head with a stone, and placed it in his creel. He rebaited the hook, rinsed his hands in the creek, and again swung the worm downstream. No trout. He tried once more, and when no fish struck, he climbed onto the bridge and crossed to the other side of the Esopus.

Standing on the bank, he swung the worm downstream and immediately caught his second trout, a 12-inch rainbow. "Zee trout, zey are rapace," he said. Two swings of his rod later, he landed a third trout, a 7-inch brown. Ordinarily he would have kept it—"Zee babeeze are zee best," he confided—but he released it because it was too small to sauté with the half-dozen 10- to 12-inch fish he planned to bring back for a feast. True to his plan, within a half hour Emile caught three more trout, and he called it quits for the day.

Lunch was boned trout, sliced tomatoes and onions, an enormous salad laced with flower blossoms, swollen loaves of freshly baked bread, carafes of red and white wine, and a hefty sampling of Belgian beers left by an eager salesman. "Zee Belgians do not 'ave zee grape," Auberge owner Madame Knab said. "So zey make beer, zee best in zee world."

Afterwards we all went outside to play petanque, a kind of French bowling game with steel balls. Every Labor Day weekend, Madame Knab told me, the Auberge was the site of the petanque championship for all the French chefs and waiters in the city. "Don't eat in zee citeee zehn," she warned. "Zee Puerto Ricans are doing zee cooking."

Alex Zagoreos, a friend of mine, was going to Paris on a business trip, and at my request he brought back a 15-foot rod just like Emile's. It cost me $200. To get the monofilament line to pass through the ceramic tunnel, I had to attach the line to the weighted needle that came with the rod. I went up to the balcony in the 20-foot foyer of our house, pointed the rod down at the floor, inserted the needle into the opening at the butt end, and gravity did the work.

No way could I cast a fly with this rod, and instead of a fly reel and fly line I put on a spinning reel with six-pound-test mono and tied on a $1/16$-ounce football-shaped jig painted red on the top half and white on the bottom and finished off with a tail of half a dozen white saddle hackles plus a few strands of fine silver Mylar. Known as the Silly Jig, it had an upright eye and shape that made it a swimming jig, unlike the ball-headed jig that goes up and down. Seth Rosenbaum, my fishing buddy, introduced the Silly Jig to me in 1963 when he used it to catch striped bass in the then impenetrable murk of the Hudson River, and he claimed that he could do barrel rolls and Immelman turns with it. I don't doubt it. Designed more than fifty years ago by a Ph.D. physics candidate named George Singer, the Silly Jig took more than a hundred species of fish around the world.

Jim Deren of the Angler's Roost in Manhattan was the first to sell painted and tied Silly Jigs, and after Jim stopped, Seth persuaded Catskill fly tier Walt Dette to handle them. They were the only jigs Walt ever painted, tied, and sold, and shortly before he died he sent me the last three dozen blanks he had.

Thus armed, I headed for the lake next door where at least a $3^1/2$-pound largemouth resided unchallenged under the dense protective cover of bushes and tree limbs that swooped low over the water. I quietly got down to lie on the ground twelve feet away from the largemouth's lair. In no way could I cast around the overgrowth or get a rod with guides through this jungle, but flat on my stomach I easily managed to poke the rod—the line inside the tunnel and the Silly Jig snug against the tip—through the bushes and under the limbs without hanging up.

When I judged that the rod tip was about a foot above the water, I carefully opened the bail on the reel, let out two feet of line, and the Silly Jig plopped into the water. I jigged it for all of three seconds. Baboom! The water exploded. I was on to the bass, and in fact fast to the bass. But how could I get the thrashing bass out of the water? I edged up on my knees and shuffled backward for fifteen feet until the bass was up on the bank and flopping on shore. What a heady sense of triumph!

I caught other bass lurking under otherwise impregnable cover, but the life of the rod came to a sudden end when I somehow fractured the lining of the ceramic tunnel and the broken pieces inside blocked the needle-carrying line. I went back to my 12-foot cane pole.

In the fall of 1994 I met Jon Shaw, visiting from England to do wildlife paintings. As I yammered on about what I was calling dapping, he looked increasingly amused. Finally, he burst out laughing and said that dapping was far more advanced than the crude version I was practicing. Nowadays, he said, the key components are a long rod—one that made my cane pole look like a pack rod—a length of fuzzy floss known as blowline or sail, a bushy palmered fly, and a breezy day. That's all I needed to hear, and I asked Jon to buy whatever I needed to bring my dapping up to date when he returned from England next spring.

While Jon was in England that winter I went through fishing books and articles to see if any Americans had ever taken notice of dapping. Very few ever had, but I did find four references that spurred me on.

First of all, John McDonald, a colleague of mine at Time Inc. who edited *The Complete Fly Fisherman: The Notes and Letters of Theodore Gordon* and wrote other books about fly fishing, reminded me about what he called not dapping but plop fishing in a memoir he wrote for *The Gordon Garland* published by the Theodore Gordon Flyfishers in 1965.

John's contribution, "Gordon and the Bergdorf Goodman Fly," dealt with an incident during the Depression. A pal of John's, Dan Bailey, a physical science teacher at Brooklyn College before he decided to head west where he opened a fly shop, earned extra

You can move the fly by raising or lowering
the rod so that the blowline catches the wind.
It's like flying a kite, only upside down.

money during those hard times by tying enormous mayfly imitations that Bergdorf Goodman, the ritzy Fifth Avenue department store, pinned to women's hats. One day while fishing near Kerhonksen in the Catskills, John lost his last fly, and fumbling for a cigarette in his pocket found one of Bailey's Bergdorf Goodman flies, a long-shanked size 1 with wings so big that it was like a small bird. He tied on the fly, and after swinging it back and forth, managed to land it "with a plop." An explosion followed as the largest brown trout he had ever seen in the East erupted from the water, dropped back down, and erupted again. The fish never again "returned below the water but, seeming to forget his species, acted the rainbow with aerial work balanced on his tail." Although the fish finally broke off with the huge fly in its nose, the experience led John to conclude that "plop fishing might be worth a try."

The other three writers who had, in one way or another, taken notice of dapping were A. J. McClane, Arnold Gingrich, and Leonard M. Wright Jr. Their notices were brief, but as you can read here, all three were dazzled by the results. Here, in chronological order of publication, are their comments.

In his 1953 book *The Practical Fly Fisherman*, McClane reported that back in the 1930s he had experimented using dental floss to catch the wind to carry his fly, a big dry spider. Despite "phenomenal" results, he said, "I can hardly recommend this as a fishing method, but with the constantly evolving refinements in tackle the day may come when superfine equipment is available."

Strangely enough, the only mention of dapping that I can find in *McClane's New Standard Fishing Encyclopedia*, which came out in 1973, is a brief passing paragraph in the entry on Ireland in which he called dapping "probably one of the most exciting forms of fishing."

In *The Joys of Trout*, which also came out in 1973, McClane's pal Gingrich wrote that one day after trout snubbed every fly he cast, he picked, out of desperation, a Strawman nymph tied by Paul Young, "a fly on which I've never taken a fish of any kind. Nor has Al McClane."

With only his 1-ounce rod, Gingrich decided to dap the nymph "along the water's edge, plop plop plop," when "a brown as long as your arm" seized it. Gingrich couldn't hold the brown, but he resumed dapping and landed a 2-pound rainbow.

In a 1974 *Sports Afield* article, later included in *Trout Maverick*, Wright described dapping with a friend's ancient English 20-foot greenheart rod, which he rigged with a light line and fine leader. Dapping and dancing a fly thirty-five feet away, no leader on the water, he wrote, "Smart, overfished trout nearly herniated themselves to grab my fly. If I'd continued to use that rod the State Conservation Department would have named me Public Enemy No. 1."

I was surprised that McDonald, McClane, Gingrich, and Wright did not follow up on dapping, but they got me steamed up with excitement, and I could hardly wait for Jon's return.

CHAPTER FOUR

Techniques
and Possibilities

JON THE DAPTIST RETURNED IN MAY WITH A ROD THAT HE BOUGHT
for me at Bennett's of Sheffield, a big British tackle dealer, along
with a 50-meter spool of Bob Church's blowline. The blowline cost
$6, the rod $200, the same as the French rod, but it was 20 feet long,
came in four 5-foot sections, and had guides. Unable to buy a tele-
scoping dapping rod, Jon assured me that the 20-foot length made it
ideal for dapping. For the record, the rod, made by Silstar, was an
Executive Class Match 600 pole designed for one of those match fishing competitions I previously mentioned. If I wished, Jon said, I could
have a much longer one, and he broke open the Bennett's catalog that
he'd brought along and, with a laugh, pointed to a $47\frac{1}{2}$-foot pole for
£3,750, or $6,000 U.S.

I declared my satisfaction with the 20-foot pole, or rod, or whatever you want to call it, and he and I immediately marched out to
the lawn for my first lesson in up-to-date dapping.

On the lawn, Jon rigged up the rod. He put an old fly reel of
mine on the butt and snaked the fly line through the guides. Next he
attached an 8-foot length of 12-pound-test monofilament to the fly

line, and then he attached an 8-foot length of blowline, which he cut from the spool of Breeze Floss Blowline from Bob Church. He knotted the floss every foot to prevent it from fraying; if it frayed it could catch in the guides and cause him to lose a fish. "When the wind is very light, we use eight feet of sail to catch the breeze," Jon said, "and when the wind is very strong, four feet."

As I later found out for myself, you can vary the length as you see fit to meet conditions. When there is no wind whatsoever, I've thought of buying a giant battery-powered electric fan and putting on 20 feet of blowline.

Jon next tied a 24-inch leader of 4-pound-test mono to the free end of the floss with a bushy palmered fly of cock's hackles on a size 10 hook.

Turning his back to the light wind wafting across the lawn, he held up the rod. The blowline caught a puff, and the fly began swirling about, now two feet above the lawn, now dropping nearly to the grass, now merrily flying high, this time in a different direction, just like a living insect, until it landed on the grass before taking flight yet again. The fly had action that the world's greatest fly fisher could not dream of duplicating.

"Dapping drives trout crazy," said Jon, who back home in Derbyshire fished private club water on the Derwent and the Wye. Well, the proof of the dapping is in the fishing, and we marched down the path through the woods to the lake to see if the moving fly would do the same to bluegills.

Standing on the dam and with the wind, which had picked up a bit, behind me, I lifted the rod high in the air, the blowline caught the breeze, and the fly flew over the water and landed thirty feet out from shore. A bluegill struck. I struck. No bluegill.

I raised the rod again so the blowline would catch the breeze. Aloft flew the fly, and I felt like the boy I used to be when I flew a kite, except that I had to lower the rod to get the fly to the water. I could see perhaps a half dozen bluegills eyeing the morsel flitting about above them. I lowered the rod to lower the fly. A bluegill struck. I struck. Again no bluegill.

"What's wrong?" I asked.

Jon said, "When a fish strikes, you should let the fish turn down with the fly before you strike, and then you strike up with your entire arm. Remember, in England when a trout strikes, you're supposed to say, 'God save the Queen' before you strike, and with a long line you can't strike just with your wrist because you'll lose the fish."

With that, when the next fish struck, I paused and said, "God bless America." I caught the fish, a 10-inch largemouth that I returned to the water. In the weeks and months that followed, using palmered drys, I caught largemouths, bluegills, and black crappies (the first crappies I ever caught on dry flies) in the lake and wild brown trout on crane fly imitations in Philipse Brook, a stream in Garrison that the locals declared too difficult to fish except with worms at night. The brook is possibly the unnamed Hudson Highlands stream where Washington Irving reported going fishless in "The Angler," the first essay in American literature about trout fishing.

I did come acropper with the 20-foot rod when I went to dap for trout in the East Branch of the Croton River. For what I mistakenly thought was ease of convenience, I assembled the rod before descending the slope to the river, and on the way down the rod kept catching on bushes and trees. If I looked sideways the rod would catch in a limb or branch up high, and if I looked up it would catch off to the side. Then when I finally wiggled myself and the rod down to riverside, the wind had shifted and was blowing in my face. I gave up, but before clambering uphill I made sure to disassemble the rod.

Another experience that should be of value to dappers: When casting a dry fly or a bass bug, I have lost many a fish when I happened to doze off or turned to look in a different direction when the fish hit. But to the contrary when I did this while dapping because nothing was happening—well, I caught almost every fish that hit because they hooked themselves.

A year later Jon the Daptist brought over a proper dapping rod, the 17-footer described in chapter 1. It cost only $75, has stood up very well over the years, and because it telescopes I don't have to worry about playing jackstraws when carrying it through woods and brush.

Other lessons learned, and I cannot repeat them often enough: Do not use fly line or a fly reel. Go to a spinning or bait casting reel. In my experience most fly fishers shudder at this very idea, and thus they never go dapping. There is a school of fly-reel fascism in this country that needs to be curbed.

Most of my dapping has been done from land, but the dapping on lakes has been done in my thirty-five-year-old Sportspal canoe. Made of thin aircraft aluminum and lined with a puffy black plastic called Ethofoam, it weighs only 36 pounds, is 14 feet long, and has a very wide 44-inch beam, making it stable. I can stand in it to fish without tipping and easily portage it, but it has no keel and catches the wind like an autumn leaf, making me feel like Beatrix Potter's Jeremy Frog. Given that I don't want the wind to blow the canoe sideways across the water and put down the fish I'm trying to catch, I slow it with a drogue, a sea anchor, which is nothing more than an old bucket tied to the canoe with a rope tied to the handle.

Apart from my own dapping experience, I really want to emphasize the possibilities that dapping has to offer. Dapping is not in its infancy in this country—the fertilized egg is still in the womb—but the maturing possibilities are limitless.

Take dapping in salt water. Bill Catherwood of Tewksbury, Massachusetts, the originator of the Giant Killers, big flies for big fish, envisioned the possibilities when he made just one attempt dapping a mackerel streamer imitation for striped bass. Jon the Daptist caught mackerel gilling with their mouths agape in a Maine harbor after a horde of anglers failed flinging jigs, streamers, plugs, and God knows what. Jon caught so many that the slimy fish kept sliding and slithering out of the bucket he brought along. His trick was dapping an imitation of a tiny, red marine worm ascending to the surface with thread he plucked from a rug.

In November of 2005, Jon called from Islamorada, Florida, to put me on the phone with Paul Ross, guide and skipper of the *Relentless*, a 48-foot custom sportfishing boat. After watching Jon dap with blowline, Captain Ross enthused, "This should open up a whole new thing for fly fishing when it gets too windy for casting. It should also work for snappers, mackerels, and tuna because when fly line lays in the water it tends to spook a lot of fish. And I can see it working on snook and tarpon in the mangroves, and it would work really good getting upwind of tailing bonefish."

One very unusual dapping technique does not call for blowline. I have yet to try it, but Art Broadie, a poacher and very deft fly fisherman known as the Black Ghost after his favorite streamer, said this when I was doing a profile about him for *Sports Illustrated*: "Now if you want your heart to jump right out of your mouth, get on a stretch of the Beaverkill, tie on a size four streamer, then six feet up the leader tie on a six-inch dropper and a dry fly. Overall the leader is 18 feet long. Flip that streamer 20 or 25 feet downstream, and hold the rod tip up so that the dry fly is hanging up in the air. You make that dry fly dance up and down. Then you just dap the water with it. I mean a trout will smash it. But where your heart jumps out of your mouth is when a 20-inch brown decides to eat the streamer that you've forgotten all about. That jars your turnips!"

CHAPTER FIVE

Flying Stoneflies

WHEN ERIC LEISER AND I WROTE *STONEFLIES FOR THE ANGLER*, we included a somewhat realistic imitation of an adult salmonfly that I named the K's Butt because the butt end of a peacock tail feather served as the buoyant body. I do not recall what prompted me to use a butt, scientifically known as a calamus; possibly the idea came from a book that I bought in 1964, Paul Young's self-published *Making and Using the Fly and Leader*, the 1938 edition, in which, as noted in chapter 9, he described quill-butt minnows. The butt concept also came to my attention later with the 1971 reprint of Vincent Marinaro's classic book *A Modern Dry Fly Code*, in which he extolled the Pontoon Hopper devised by Charlie Craighead and Bill Bennett of the Harrisburg Fly-Fishers' Club.

Eric and I sent K's Butts to anglers we knew for field testing, and, in the most vivid account we received, Charlie Brooks wrote that on the Madison River below the Varney Bridge, brown trout up to five pounds "would chase the damn fly downstream, hit it going like an express train, and just keep on going when they felt the hook. Some were too big to force back upstream even with 12-pound-test leaders. We hooked maybe forty, landed about fifteen, all 18 inches or smaller. We just couldn't handle the big fish (4- to 5-pounders) in that fast water. The fast tearing runs just shook my old 1495 Medalist reel apart. Screws all came loose, lost one. Damnedest day I ever had with running trout."

Later, in *The Orvis Guide to Prospecting for Trout*, Tom Rosenbauer called the K's Butts "monstrous" imitations, "horrible things to tie," but luckily for him and Mark Bressler, a Wyoming rancher and friend, he went on to report he had some with him one day when they fished the Upper New Fork. "Standing on the bank," Rosenbauer wrote, "beside a pool that was too deep and too fast to wade, I saw brown trout 16 to 22 inches come up from five feet below the surface to nail that fly. It was like fishing with a bass bug, and on a 5-weight rod the casting wasn't much fun—but the strike and the fight were worth the trouble."

Others reported great success in taking trout, as well as small-mouth and largemouth bass, in lakes that wouldn't know a *Pteronarcys californica* from a pontificating Californian. Even so, the first K's Butts had a flaw. Trout could puncture the peacock butt end with their teeth and sink it.

What follows is, as advertising copywriters would say, the New and Improved K's Butt that should, knock wood, float forever, whether cast or dapped, impervious to all teeth except those of a barracuda.

The K's Butt does take time to tie, but it's worth it, and as George F. Grant wrote in *The Master Fly Weaver*, "There is one word that the amateur flytier should immediately eliminate from his vocabulary, and that word is 'speed.'" What counts is how fish respond. No one asked Michelangelo how long it took to paint the ceiling of the Sistine Chapel or Tolstoy to write *War and Peace*.

The K's Butt has a head-to-tail body with a solid quill shaft, also known as a rachis, inserted through the very durable butt end of a wing or tail feather from a Canada goose, turkey, pheasant, or other large bird. The shaft protrudes through both the front and rear of the

If you immerse a peeled quill strip in hot water, you can then wrap it around an underbody to simulate the abdominal segments of an insect (marking the back and belly in different colors) or shrimp, and you can cut pieces from a strip for antennae, legs, claws, and wing cases.

butt; this not only adds durability to the fly, the squarish protruding ends also serve as tier-friendly platforms for the tail end and head of the fly.

The insertion of a solid quill shaft inside a hollow butt has wide application. By varying the length and width of the shaft and butt, you can size them to imitate the adults of other insects besides stoneflies, such as mayflies, dragonflies, damselflies, grasshoppers, dobsonflies, crane flies, and caddis flies, as well as shrimp and minnows, as noted in later chapters. Should you want to go small, use the wing or tail feathers from a starling, an unprotected bird whose array of feathers has earned it the nickname in Britain of the fly-dresser's friend.

Although I now rarely use a peacock butt as the body for a fly, I have other uses for the peacock shaft itself. I start by peeling footlong, flexible strips from the glossy side above the butt. This horny material composed of keratin, the same substance found in human

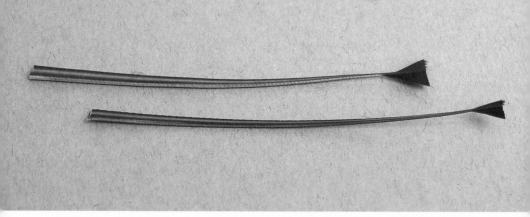

You can use wing and tail feathers from other birds. For instance, I trim the tip of Canada goose wing and tail feathers to make tiny brushes that I use to apply Krazy Glue and colored lacquers. Where there's a quill, there's a way.

fingernails, resembles the chitinous "skin" of an insect or crustacean, and as shown here, it can be dyed or colored with a permanent marking pen.

The K's Butt Flying Golden Stone is a generic imitation of any number of the family Perlidae (genus *Acroneuria, Agnetina, Classenia, Hesperoperla,* et al.), found across North America. Like some duck decoy carvers, I make my Golden Stone a slight bit larger than life because I adhere to the dapping dictum of G. P. R. Balfour-Kinnear, who, in *A Boy Goes Trouting*, declared that the "fly must be a worthwhile prize to make a trout come for it from any distance."

MATERIALS

Hook:	Tiemco 200R, size 6
Upright hook eye:	Mustad 32755 Aberdeen jig hook, size 12, eye half only
Tying threads:	Danville waxed Flymaster, 6/0, yellow
Outer body:	Butt end Canada goose primary feather
Inner body:	Solid quill shaft from same feather
Tail section:	Protruding end of solid quill shaft

Tails:	Two dark brown hog bristles
Abdominal segments:	Spiraled black thread
Thorax:	Flat cork sheet
Head:	Protruding front of quill shaft
Eyes:	Burnt 50-pound-test mono
Antennae:	Two dark brown hog bristles
Legs:	Brown Canada goose biots
Wings:	Etha-Wing or four epoxied mallard flank feathers

Plus Krazy Glue and Sally Hansen's Hard As Nails clear nail polish (for head cement) where applicable.

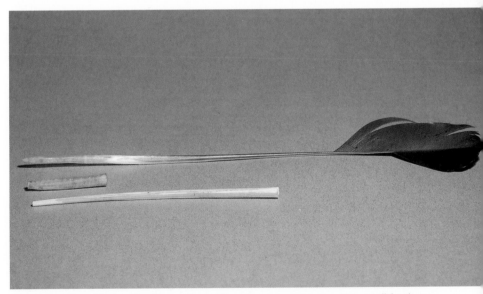

Step 1. After stripping the fibers from a Canada goose primary wing or tail feather, cut off a butt, about 1¼ inches long, and a length of shaft, and dye both or color them yellow with a permanent marker.

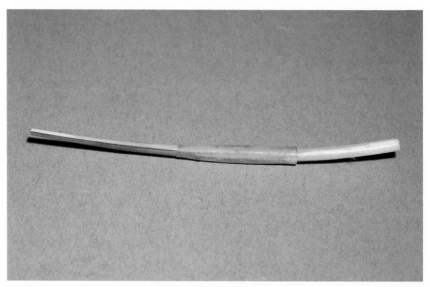

Step 2. After clipping open a small hole at the end of the butt, remove the pith, and insert the shaft through the front of the butt and out the rear for a snug fit.

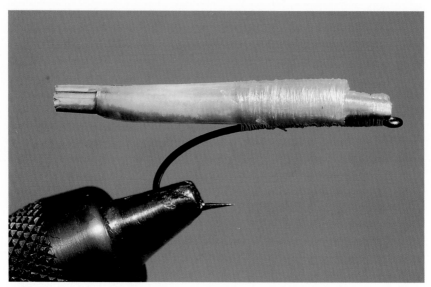

Step 3. Cut the excess shaft from the front and rear, leaving space for the head and tail. Flatten the head with pliers, tie it on the hook, secure with Krazy Glue, and let dry.

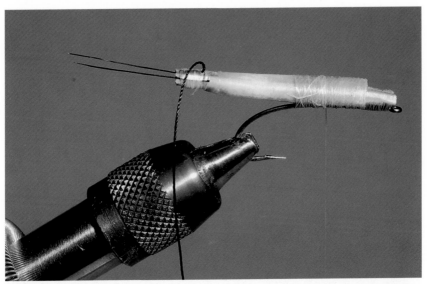

Step 4. Tie in the tails and black thread that will mark the segments, and secure them with nail polish.

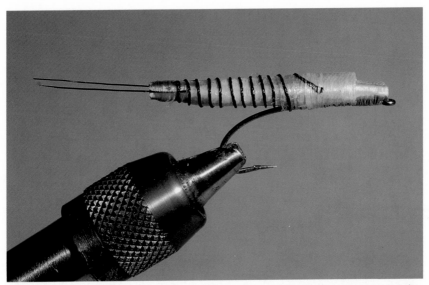

Step 5. Spiral the black thread forward to mark ten abdominal segments, stopping where the thorax begins. Coat the black thread, tie it down, and coat the body with nail polish.

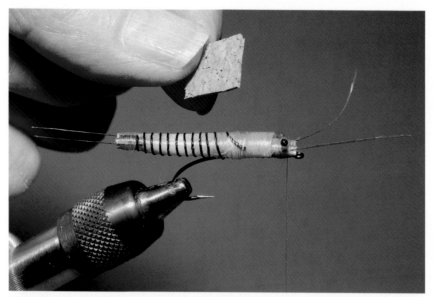

Step 6. Continue forward with yellow tying thread, and tie in the mono eyes with figure-eight turns and the antennae on each side. Place the flat cork sheet on the body to build up the thorax.

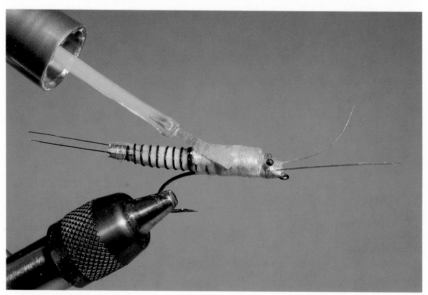

Step 7. Tie down the thorax, and coat it and the head with nail polish.

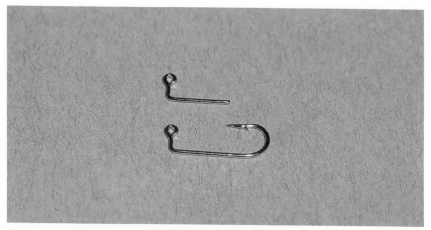

Step 8. Use shears to cut an upright jig hook in half.

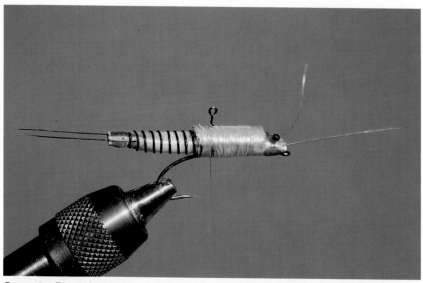

Step 9. Place the shank of the jig hook, eye upright, at about the middle of the thorax, and make enough turns of the tying thread to *temporarily* secure the shank on the thorax. Remove the fly from the vise. Insert a line in the eye and lift the fly in the air by the line to find its center of gravity. If the fly is parallel to the ground, you've found it. If not, reinsert the fly in the vise and shift the shank backward or forward until you find it. Secure the jig shank with Krazy Glue, and let dry.

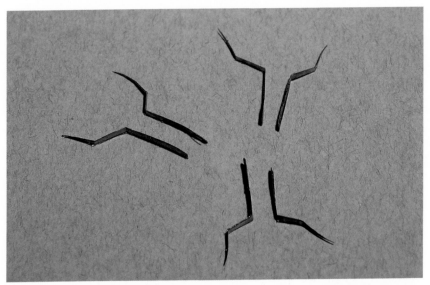

Step 10. Use tweezers or hackle pliers to bend goose biots to form legs. Bend each biot in half, then bend the lower half in half again to mark the thigh, femur, and tibia, and coat with Krazy Glue to retain the shape. I do dozens of legs ahead of time so that I do not have to stop and wait for the Krazy Glue to dry whenever I tie this fly. I do the same with other materials that would otherwise hold up tying, such as coating mallard flank feathers with epoxy for wings.

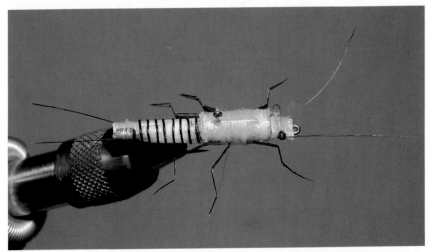

Step 11. Tie in the legs, starting with the rear pair, and finishing with the front pair. Tie off and cut the tying thread, and coat the fly with nail polish.

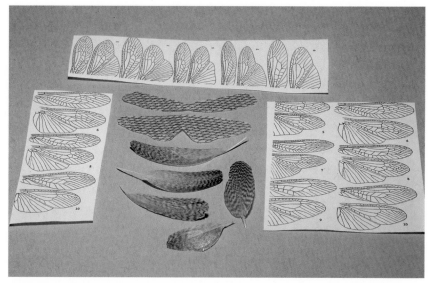

Step 12. Cut the front and rear pair of wings from Etha-Wing using templates or individual wings from epoxied mallard flank feathers. It's hard to find large enough flank feathers, so I often use Etha-Wing. I epoxy a flank feather by gripping the center stem with hackle pliers and dragging both sides of the feather through five-minute epoxy. I then immediately skim off as much epoxy as possible with a toothpick before letting the feather dry.

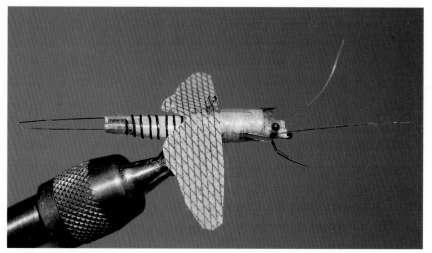

Step 13. Cut a small slit in the rear pair of Etha-Wing wings, position the slit above the upright eye, press the wings down, secure with Krazy Glue, and let dry.

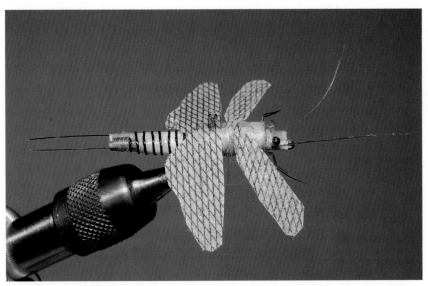

Step 14. Position front wing ahead of rear wing, place down, secure with Krazy Glue, let dry, and voila! Go dapping with the K's Butt Flying Golden Stone.

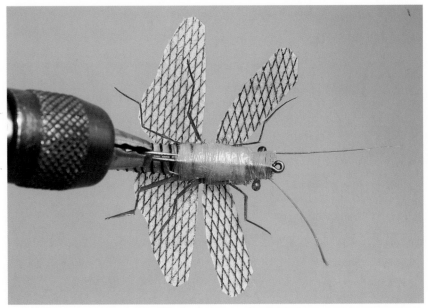

What the trout sees flying above.

The Flying K's Butt Golden Stone with epoxied wings of mallard flank feathers and egg sac—the "steak and eggs" version.

Again, what the trout sees.

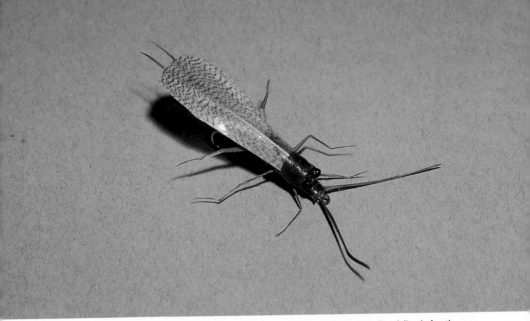

The salmonfly, *Pteronarcys californica,* with just one epoxied mallard flank feather trimmed to shape and laid flat over the back. This feather imitates all four wings that a stonefly folds together as one when it is at rest. No need to tie in the upright jig hook for dapping. I warn you that this style imitation will dangle by the nose, but you'll certainly take trout casting it.

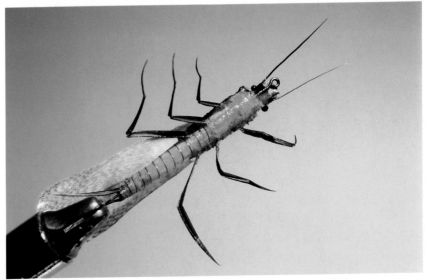

A salmonfly down on the water from the trout's point of view.

CHAPTER SIX

Flying Dragonflies

Today I saw the dragonfly
Come from the wells where he did lie.
An inner impulse rent the veil
Of his old husk, from head to tail
Came out clear plates of sapphire mail.
He dried his wings: like gauze they grew;
Thro' crofts and pastures wet with dew
A living flash of light he flew.

—Tennyson

SOME FORTY YEARS AGO, HARRY DARBEE KINDLY GAVE ME MY first tying lessons, and dragonflies were the first insects that I seriously sought to duplicate. The dragonflies then were not for trout but for largemouth and smallmouth bass, and before I attempted to tie even one I read as much as I could about dragonflies.

Dragonflies are part of the order Odonata, Greek for "toothed," the only insect order that does not include "pter," Greek for "wings," in its name. The order has two suborders, the Anisoptera ("equal wings"), or dragonflies, that hold their wings horizontally at rest, and the Zygoptera ("yoke wings"), or damselflies, that hold their wings upright and together at rest.

Among the books on aquatic insects that I acquired, and I must have more than a hundred, was R. J. Tillyard's masterwork, *The*

Biology of Dragonflies, published in 1917 by the Cambridge University Press. I often write in the date when I buy a book, and I see that I marked my first dragonfly purchase, a copy of "The Odonata or Dragonflies of Connecticut" by Philip Giarman as November 1963, and that I bought *A Manual of the Dragonflies of North America (Anisoptera)* by James G. Needham and Minter J. Westfall in November 1964. I went on to buy a number of out-of-print scientific papers and journals by dragonfly authorities, including a batch by Baron Edmund de Selys Longchamps, a nineteenth- and early-twentieth-century Belgian statesman whose insect collection was world famous. I even went so far as to conduct a brief correspondence with a Dr. S. Asahina, editor of a Japanese journal called *Tombo*, Japanese for "dragonfly."

Too much? Yes, possibly, but whenever I become interested in an animal, curiosity seizes me and I am compelled to gather as much intelligence as I can about the animal's physiology and life history. Too many fly fishers don't do this, and that's a shame because it gives you an edge when fishing. And don't we all want that?

In addition to the scientific literature, I bought a butterfly net from Ward's in Rochester, New York, and set about collecting dragonflies on the wing even before tying a fly. One huge dragonfly that particularly intrigued me was *Epiaeschna (Aeshna) heros*, which reaches a length of ninety-one millimeters, about five inches. Its Greek generic name means "near ugly" and its specific name "warrior." There was a drawing of this warrior in a curious book I bought from the Gilman brothers in Crompond, New York, then the greatest out-of-print bookseller in the United States and possibly the world. Published by D. Appleton and Company in 1890, *Dragon Flies vs. Mosquitoes* is a collection of essays by "Working Entomologists" with an introduction by Robert H. Lamborn, Ph.D., who offered, through the agency of the American Museum of Natural History, prizes of $150, $30, and $20 to the authors of the three best essays on how to raise dragonflies to eat mosquitoes, inspired in good part by the successful raising of hatchery fish.

MOSQUITO HAWKS, OR DRAGON FLIES.

1. ANAX JUNIUS.   2. ÆSCHNA HEROS.

From Dragon Flies vs. Mosquitoes

Alas, I had no luck in spotting *heros*, and so I focused on *Anax junius*, the other large dragonfly pictured in the book. Its name means "king of June," and it was common in the Hudson Valley where I lived. As a matter of fact, it is commonly found throughout North America, the West Indies, the Hawaiian Islands, and the west coast of Asia, and I believed that an imitation of a captive specimen would entice a bass, or maybe even a trout, beyond my dreams.

I had no luck with the net, though. One swipe of it, and any *junius* I saw would zoom at least six stories high into the sky. Dragonflies have compound eyes that give them remarkable vision, possibly the best in the insect world, because of the number of individual eyes, ommatidia, they contain. According to Ross E. Hutchins, professor emeritus of entomology at Mississippi State, the compound eye of a house fly has about 4,000 ommatidia, while a big dragonfly may have as many as 28,000. On the advice of an entomologist friend, Dominick Pirone, who became a professor of ecology at Manhattan College, I added another weapon to my collecting arsenal, an oil squirt can loaded with soapy water. A jet of soapy water, Dom said, would temporarily down *junius* so that I could examine it and take a color picture before it flew away. Again no luck. Trying to down one with an oil squirt can shooting a jet of soapy water was like trying to bring down a helicopter gunship with a slingshot.

I finally wrote to a dragonfly specialist, and he kindly sent me a dried specimen. The colors had faded, but I was able to duplicate them by following the description in Needham and Westfall's monograph.

It took several days to tie, or rather construct, the imitation. I wound deer hair on a long-shank hook, clipped it to shape, left a ball for the head and a hump for the thorax, and soaked all with Sally Hansen's nail polish. When the polish began to dry, I squeezed the deer hair half a dozen times to the shapes I wanted; I wrapped the abdomen and thorax in raffia; and I delineated the abdominal segments by individually encircling them with fine black thread. Two or three days passed before I tied on the four extended wings, stiff, light brown hackle from the neck of a rooster. I used lacquer to paint the green, yellow, brown, and black parts of the body to simulate *junius*.

Proud of my creation, I attached it to the end of the leader of my 9-foot bass bugging rod, and accompanied by a fishing pal, Ronald Dagon, an Arctic ecologist then at the New York Botanical Garden, I headed off on a sunny June afternoon to Mrs. Willard Brinton's private pond, which I had permission to fish. For some reason, Dagon brought my butterfly net with him to the pond, and while I stood on the shore, idly jiggling my imitation, pondering where to cast, suddenly, from nowhere, a real-life *A. junius* swooped in to kill or copulate with my fly.

With a quick turn of the net Dagon captured it, and for the first time I was able to examine a live specimen in all its glittering glory. Forget about catching a fish—though this imitation later caught its share—devising a fly that caught a living fly with 28,000 eyes is the greatest compliment that any fly tier could ever hope for.

That encounter spurred me into using realistic imitations to decoy dragonflies as though they were ducks. In time I became so intrigued, so involved with dragonflies that I wrote an outdoors column about them for *The New York Times*. When the column appeared I read, to my dismay, that wherever I had written "entomologist" or "entomology," the column said "etymologist" and "etymology," including an account of "etymologist" Ross Hutchins, who measured the aerial speed of dragonflies by clocking them while following them in a light plane. Embarrassed, mortified, and chagrined, I immediately called the copy editor who had put the column to press. "But that's what you sent us," he said. "Hell, no!" I exclaimed. "You changed it! I'm a member of the New York Entomological Society, not the Etymological Society!"

"What's the difference?" he asked. Stunned, I said, "Entomology refers to the study of insects. Etymology is the study of words." "Oh," he said.

Bad enough, but what really stunned me is that not one of the million-plus reputedly highly educated readers of *The New York Times* wrote to ask why an etymologist would go up in a plane to measure the speed of dragonflies.

Not long ago, thanks to Dick Dahlgren, I found another dragonfly enthusiast as well as a bizarre dapper of sorts. He is Harry Smith, 78, and he lives in Santa Ana, California, near Disneyland.

Harry's bizarre dapping began five years ago after he gave up fishing for steelhead and trout to go after the largemouth bass hiding under heavy shoreline brush in a lake. No fly fisher would even think of venturing into such a jungle, but Harry did by quietly using a float tube. On his first voyage in the tube, he heard bass splashing under some heavy brush. As a lifelong student of hatches, he was puzzled because none was going on. What could the bass be after? He watched and watched, and finally he saw what was going on. Two birds were taking turns flying in and out from some low-lying branches next to the shore, feeding their young in a nest, and their constant flying back and forth had aroused the bass below.

Back home Harry tied the realistic feather bird shown here. Like me, he tied it so that his bird flew upright rather than dangle down by the nose.

Back at the lake, the bird on a 25-pound-test leader (the bass were in heavy cover) three inches below the tip of his 8-foot, 6-weight fly rod, Harry embarked in the float tube and quietly foot-paddled his way to the nest site. Extending his rod, he made the bird hippity-hop from branch to branch. The bass exploded.

He released them all, and back home he tied up a new bird without a hook (the bird with the hook also caught branches as well as bass) and returned to the lake to see how many times he could get bass to strike. "Increased my strike ratio by the hundreds," he told me. "I have had up to thirty-five strikes from one fish."

Harry did more. He took a Neoprene Glacier Glove, glued Velcro on the five fingers, secured five 2-foot-long rod tips to each of the five fingers, and put five hookless birds on the end of five 3-inch

Harry's Hippity-Hop Bird

leaders. Bass went crazy. "Five too heavy," Harry says. He cut back to three rod tips. Bass still went bonzo.

Next he created a hookless shad imitation: deer hair body with marabou, quickly dapped from side to side with the 8-foot, 6-inch rod with a soft tip that can, in Harry's words, "shake that shad." Harry generated a feeding frenzy. I told him that I was dapping with blow-line. He scoffed: "You're fishing open water. I'm not. You're driving an Edsel, and I'm flying a jet. I'm fishing virgin water. Nobody fish-es the water I fish. The average fly fisherman has to throw a fly, but they can't with the heavy cover, and that's where the fish are."

Harry is now fishing dragonflies, one at a time, and unlike the shad, they never touch the water. "I'm fishing in the air," he said. "I want to see what happens." One thing he wants to see is how far a bass will come out of the water for a dragonfly. The record so far is three feet. Although he does not want a bass to catch the dragonfly, to his regret they sometimes do. Why the regret? "I'm old, I'm tired, tired of getting my hands wet. I've had my hands in so much water I haven't washed them in years. All my life I've been trying to get fish to take my fly. Now I don't want them to get it."

One of the dragonflies I tie is *Sympterum rubicundulum*, whose scientific names come from the Greek, *sympiedgo*, "to press together," because of its narrow abdomen, and the Latin, *rubicundulus*, "somewhat ruddy," for its color. In everyday American, it's known as the Ruby Meadowhawk. Actually, because differences are so slight, the imitation could be any one of about a dozen in the genus found across North America (plus about another forty species in the North Temperate Zone in the other parts of the planet). It is usually a fall species, but some emerge as early as June. While generally considered a pond denizen, it has been reported on the wing near streams.

Total length of body is 37 or 38 millimeters, of which the abdomen measures 21 to 25 millimeters. The length of the hind wing is 26 to 30 millimeters; its width is 9 millimeters.

A key point in tying on the body for this pattern is to leave sufficient space on the front of the hook shank for the dragonfly's head.

MATERIALS

Hook:	Tiemco 3761, size 4
Thread:	Danville waxed Flymaster red, 6/0, for body; Danville waxed Flymaster black, 6/0, for body segmentation and head
Abdomen and thorax:	Quill butt end with solid quill shaft, protruding only at tail, not at head
Permanent marker for body:	Red Pantone 192-T

Permanent markers for wing:	Same red Pantone for pterostigma; brown Pantone 471-T for brownish flush extending from wing bases
Segmentation:	Spiraled Danville waxed Flymaster black thread, 6/0
Legs:	Black or dark brown hog bristle bent to shape
Head:	Black wool

Plus Sally Hansen's Hard as Nails polish and Krazy Glue

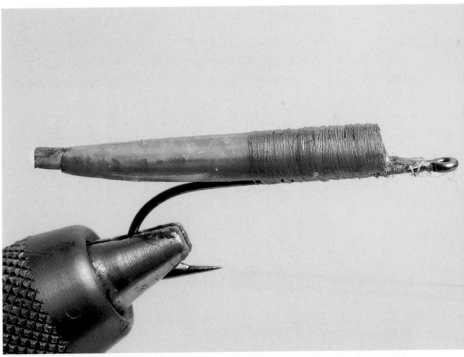

Step 1. Repeat tying steps 1, 2, and 3 for the K's Butt Flying Golden Stone. Note: Many of the tying steps for the Flying Dragonfly are the same. Leave a portion of the solid quill shaft protruding at the rear, but leave none at the front. Insert the hook in the vise, place the quill body on top of the shank, leaving space for the wool head, tie down at the thorax, secure with Krazy Glue, and let dry.

Step 2. Tie in a strand of black wool with black thread, and wind to form the head, bigger in the rear than at the front, using the hook eye as a stopping point and securing the wool in place after every few turns with black thread and nail polish. Tie off the head, remove the hook from the vise, apply Krazy Glue to the head, and let dry.

Step 3. Take shears to cut off the hook eye and shape the head, apply Krazy Glue where needed, and let dry.

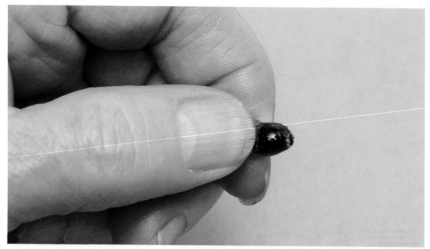

The head should look like this.

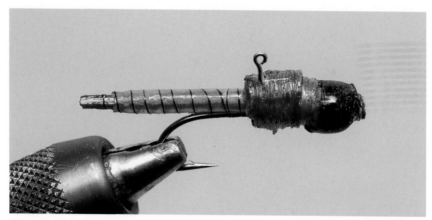

Step 4. As with the K's Butt Flying Golden Stone, tie in black thread to mark the ten abdominal segments, spiral the black thread forward, stopping where the thorax begins, and coat the black thread and body with nail polish. Use red thread to tie down not one but two pieces of flat cork sheeting, the longer piece first with the shorter piece's rear end immediately above the rear end of the first piece to simulate the slanting humped thorax of the dragonfly. Take the Mustad Aberdeen jig hook, cut it in half with shears, and place the shank of the jig hook with the eye upright at about the middle of the thorax. Make enough turns of tying thread to test for the center of gravity before tying down the shank, securing it with Krazy Glue, and letting it dry.

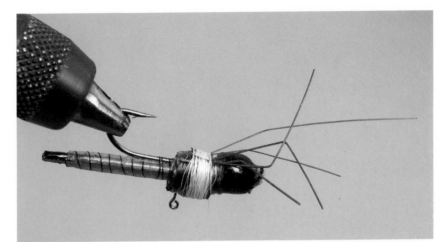

Step 5. Place the fly in the vise upside down, tie in six bent (heated) legs thrusting forward from the thorax to imitate the dragonfly's "basket catch," tie off the thread, and apply nail polish. I had to use white thread after running out of red thread, but no problem: I colored the thread with red Pantone 192-T.

Step 6. As with the K's Butt Flying Golden Stone, cut two pairs of Etha-Wings, this time dragonfly-size, place a drop of Krazy Glue on the back, press down the rear wings, and repeat with the front wings. With a red permanent marker, mark the pterostigmata on the wing tips, and use a brown permanent marker to shade the wings. As an added flourish, you can add to the imitation by touching the front of the head with yellow lacquer.

Here is an eleven-year-old dapped version of S. rubicundulum *with epoxied mallard wings, the front pair down, the second pair up, just the way a dragonfly alternates the pairs in flight. Although I did not color the wings, fish went after it.*

Another dragonfly that I tie is the male of Libellula pulchella, *from* libella, *Latin for "water level," presumably because dragonflies in this genus generally fly at a given level around a pond or lake; and the Latin* pulchellus, *"beautiful." It is commonly known as the Twelve Spot because of the dozen dark blotches on the wings. The species occurs throughout the contiguous forty-eight states and part of Canada.*

The tying steps and materials are practically identical to those for S. rubicundulum, *except for the grizzly feather wings and—more importantly—the upright hook on top of the back. Note how the shank of the upright hook, its eye sheared off, fits in the groove of the solid quill shaft where it is tied down and secured with Krazy Glue. This allows this dragonfly to be dapped the old-fashioned way right on top of lily pads and emergent vegetation without snagging.*

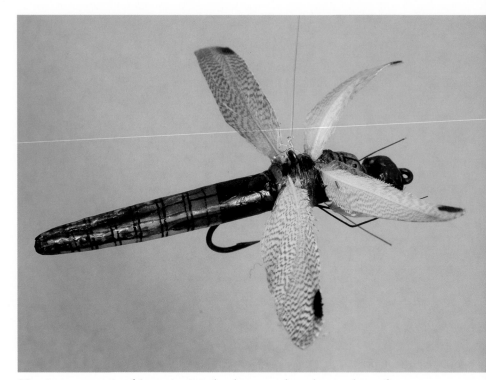

Here is a veteran tie of Anax junius *that has gone through several transformations since it was first tied for casting more than thirty years ago. In fact, it appeared in* The Fly-Tyer's Almanac *with horse hair wings, and before that it had white hackle wings. Now adapted for dapping with an upright hook eye in the midthorax, it has hog bristle legs and mallard flank feather wings glued to clear plastic. The original India-ink segmentation on the abdomen still holds up despite the passage of decades, and the same goes for the lacquered deer hair thorax and head. Not bad, but I've been thinking about snipping the hook from the midbottom and tying one on top of the back as with* Libellula pulchella.

Harry Smith's hookless dragonfly for "air fishing" has an abdomen of braided nylon rope, a thorax of sheet packing foam, Rubber Silly Legs, five-minute epoxy eyes, and photocopied wings of Mylar.

SEVEN

Disrespected
Crane Flies

All [crane flies] are great favourites for dapping, and sometimes in the
summer they get blown on to the water in very large quantities, when
trout go mad over them.

　　　　　　—A. Courtney Williams, *Trout Flies* (London, 1932)

IN THIS COUNTRY, ALAS, CRANE FLIES ARE THE RODNEY DANGERFIELD of insects. They don't get no respect from entomologists who see no money in them. They don't get no respect from folks who swat them because they're mistaken for giant mosquitoes. And they don't get no respect from anglers unaware of their importance, despite the fact that trout and bass will gorge themselves on them whenever they have the chance.

　Even though crane flies are disrespected, my number one dapping fly is an imitation of a large adult crane fly, *Tipula abdominalis.* Crane flies proper, as distinguished from closely related insects known as "phantom crane flies" and "winter crane flies," belong to the Tipulidae family. The family name comes from *tipula*, Latin for "water spider," because of the way the resting adult extends its extraordinarily long legs like a spider. The common name comes from the stiltlike legs, which resemble those on a crane and which break off very easily. The legs inspired the anonymous poet laureate of crane flies to pen this couplet:

"My six long legs, all here and there,

Oppress my bosom with despair."

Actually, the loss of a leg, even three or four legs, can be advantageous, allowing the crane fly to escape from a predator's clutches.

Few insects are more widely distributed on the planet: Crane flies are found from the tropics to Greenland, only eight degrees shy of the North Pole, and from sea level to mountains 11,000 feet high. Most larvae are aquatic or semiaquatic, and others live in a moist land environment with damp soil and decaying vegetation.

A typical female lays 150 to 200 eggs, and if only two hatch and manage to reproduce, the species perpetuates itself. The other eggs, larvae, and adults that don't succumb to drought, sudden freezes, or other vagaries of nature end up as food for insects, fishes, amphibians, birds, and other animals. The larvae are the major food for breeding shorebirds in the tundra of northern Alaska and starlings in Scotland. Many other predators undoubtedly depend on the larval populations, which can reach truly astronomic levels. Back in the 1930s, J. Speed Rogers of the University of Michigan calculated that the total weight of the larvae in the university's 1,268-acre George Reserve "can hardly be less, and may well be greater, than that of the deer."

Despite this, Rogers wrote, "The crane flies are usually regarded as a definitely minor group, neglected by the general collector and ignored in nearly all ecological surveys." That still holds. As George W. Byers at the University of Kansas states, "Crane fly biology is a vast and only slightly explored field, much in need of interested students."

The aquatic larvae are mainly burrowers and generally unavailable as prey, except when washed downstream by a spate. Some larvae have a transparent thin skin, while others have a tough skin and are called leather jackets by bait fishermen. A few species pupate and hatch in the water, but the majority migrate to land to pupate before emerging.

Some larvae are carnivorous, but the majority are detritivores, and they perform an important role in processing leaf litter. In wooded parts of the country, streams derive most of their energy from an annual event that is so obvious, yet so subtle, that most people do not comprehend its significance. It is the leaf drop in the autumn, the greatest transfer of energy in the course of the year. Some leaves fall directly into the stream, others are blown in, and, after immersion and colonization by bacteria and fungi, they serve as a storehouse of organic carbon, calcium, nitrogen, magnesium, phosphorus, and other nutrients, all free for the taking by crane fly larvae and a host of other detritivores, among them many mayfly and stonefly nymphs and caddis larvae.

Probably no insects present a more startling difference in appearance than do larval and adult crane flies. Many larvae, nicknamed "water worms," are fat, with obscenely bloated bodies. In contrast, the adults have slender bodies with their "six long legs, all here and there." It's as though Orson Welles metamorphosed into Tommy Tune.

Most adults live only a few days, and they are most active at dusk or during the day after a rain shower. Out of necessity, adults are drawn to water and a humid environment. Although the great majority of species do not eat, they must drink water to avoid dehydration. It doesn't take much to have that happen. In as little as two hours water loss can cause the numerous species in the genus *Tipula* to lose up to 10 percent of their body weight in an air temperature of 68 degrees and a relative humidity of 60 percent.

The slender bodies of the adults put them at the mercy of the wind, and they can be easily blown onto the surface of a stream or lake. Almost every adult crane fly, no matter where it lives in the larval stage, is likely to be found near flowing or standing water. Thus, as Charles Paul Alexander wrote in his classic two-volume study, *The Crane-Flies of New York*: "Fragments of the adult flies are often found in the stomach contents of fish, notably species of trout, most of these pieces being individuals that had fallen into the water or were captured while newly transformed."

When a hatch is on, the numbers can be enormous. I remember the September day I attended a Washington Redskins practice with the team owner, Jack Kent Cooke. A bit of an odd character, Cooke could be reclusive, but *Sports Illustrated* hoped that I could get him to open up for a story. We were standing on a sideline watching the offense when I suddenly happened to look down and saw hundreds, if not thousands, of very big crane flies, probably *Tipula abdominalis*, cartwheeling across the field blown by the wind. "Look at that!" I exclaimed. "Look at what?" asked Cooke. "All these crane flies," I said, pointing down at them. He shot me a strange look, and it immediately dawned on me that Cooke had thought that I'd spotted a lineman offside or a receiver running the wrong pattern. But crane flies? I knew I'd blown it. Cooke clammed up, and I caught the train back to New York.

Besides myself, I know of only three other American crane fly enthusiasts: Dick Dahlgren (Harry Smith's pal); Howard Bartholomew of Middleburgh, New York, a founding member of the Royal American Dapping Club; and Paul Schmookler of Westborough, Massachusetts, who says, "Most fly fishermen pay no attention to crane fly adults. I think it's basically because mayflies, stoneflies, and caddisflies have gotten a lot of coverage, and crane flies not very much. They've been forgotten."

Dick Dahlgren became a dapper with the forgotten crane fly in 2002, a year after I sent him some crane fly imitations and a length of blowline. I did this because I always want others to test a new fly I have tied or try a new way of fishing like dapping to let me know if it works. Dick emailed me back:

"Mid-August, 2003. Big Lost River in central Idaho, eleven in the morning and already hot. Me knee deep in this cool western stream. Fishing successfully for an hour using a Mackay Special, weirdest thing you ever did see; reddish brown horsehair, long shanked size 8 or 10, stiff sparse wings, woven orange or green abdomen, locals always fish it wet.

"Then the breeze stiffened, still hot, gusting to 20 mph, the scary kind of wind that puts fear in the hearts of the local USFS fire crews, the kind of wind that can burn a forest in a few hours. Got out, went back to the cabin for a sandwich. I thought, well I never tried your dapping system, and I took down the envelope you sent the year before, dumped out the contents: several nicely tied crane flies, some long length of blowline, and your instructions on what to do.

"You said I needed a stiff breeze. Okay. I cut back on the tippet, tied on about six feet of the blowline and added another section of tippet on the end of that. Tied on a crane fly, and back out I went.

"I knew the perfect spot upstream. About a third of a mile was a narrow fast-flowing section, cottonwoods on one side, an alfalfa field on the other, a hundred yards long, maybe forty feet wide. I call it the Rock Garden because that's what it is: dozens of basketball-size rocks in a run at the head of the pool, a grocery store for dozens of large hungry trout.

"Upstream I went, ducking behind a guide and his client, two Orvistonians, with looks of disgust to my 'Howdy,' and ''Scuse me,' and waded in at the top of the Rock Garden. The Orvistonians were still looking at me a hundred yards distant. They didn't like my costume; I'd heard one little comment after I passed, but, hey, what's wrong with shorts, a lime green, orange, and blue Hawaiian shirt, a US Navy baseball cap with USNS Mercy T-AH19 in gold letters, red high-top patent leather basketball shoes, and a raunchy old fishing vest?

"I was knee deep in the current, wind behind me blowing downstream, dozens of rock-bulging pocket water targets fifty feet below me. I stripped out twenty feet of line, held my rod high, and let go of the crane fly. The wind took it up and away. I watched the blowline and the fly dance in the air; suddenly the fly hit the water in front of a rock, lifted off in an instant, and came down just as quick-ly. A foot-long rainbow exploded. I was so startled I missed the strike.

"This was my first, uh, cast? Attempt? Meanwhile the blowline was whipping around in the wind. I watched it buck and sail, then dive, and the fly bounced down by another rock. Another explosion. This time I hooked the fish, played him to the side. This 'bow was a beautiful heavy-shouldered 18-incher.

"The action went like this for close to an hour. I finally stopped striking and watched the fish react. Well, not entirely. I wanted to see if one of the big guys would rush the fly the same way as the little 18-incher. Off to the side was a narrow deep slot between two sub-merged large rocks. There is always a big fish lurking there. This time I was more deliberate, letting the crane fly dance, but not touching the water until it was above the right spot.

"Down the fly went, touching the water exactly where I wanted it. A 24-inch perfectly shaped hen slashed the surface and took it. The fish jumped a half dozen times and made a long run downstream, ending about four rod lengths from the two Orvistonians. I guided her into the shallows, slipped the fly out without touching her and watched her scoot away.

"The breeze was dying, and I'd had more than enough. So I smiled at the Orvistonians as I passed, headed back to the cabin for an afternoon cigar and a wee nip of a good single malt scotch. I thought I'd write you about my killer day, my first experience with dapping."

In Britain and Ireland, crane flies do get respect from fly fishers. There they are known as daddy-longlegs, the name we use for the eight-leg arachnids, related to spiders, that the Brits call harvestmen. In Britain, "fishing the daddy," or "fishing the Harry," another nick-name for crane flies, both dry and wet, is standard practice, and there are a number of patterns with names that sound as if they belong in an old Peter Sellers or Terry Thomas comedy, such as Demented Daddy, Drowning Daddy, and Wet Daddy.

"I am incredibly surprised that the crane fly isn't recognized in the States," says Jon the Baptist. "At home I'd say it's the second most important hatch after the mayfly." In fact, as I discovered while reading the catalogs of some British dealers offering fly-tying materials, the crane fly with pheasant-tail fiber legs is in such demand that legs are sold already knotted.

"The daddy-longlegs in England usually doesn't hatch until late August or September," Jon notes, "and then there's a big hatch, but here in New York I've seen them hatching in early June. In fact, I went around to a friend's pond the other day [in early June] with my dapping rod and put a great big daddy-longlegs on, and straightaway a bass came up and smashed it on the surface.

"I always bring a whole boxful of daddy imitations with me to fish because they're so effective, especially dapping, but fishing them in the regular dry-fly manner is extremely effective, too, for trout, bass, or panfish. You can twitch them just to make a little bit of a riffle or a wake. Very often the movement will attract a fish's attention. Often I will just give it a little jerk so that it makes a wake and then let it sit there. You can use it on any water, still or rough. They're very good on a reservoir, and they are very good on the river. You can even let the dry daddy get waterlogged and sink below the surface. This is certainly one of the most effective flies that I've fished, especially at dusk or in the early morning, but fish will take them all day long in Britain. I've also used them in Wyoming, and I caught trout easily on them. The trout took them very confidently."

Inasmuch as the Tipulidae constitute the largest family in the Diptera, with 15,000 species described worldwide, it would seem that crane flies had attracted an army of entomologists. Not so at all.

Incredibly enough, one man alone, Charles Paul Alexander, described and scientifically named more than 10,000 crane flies in more than a thousand papers and books, and no scientist in the world has ever come close to describing that number of new species in a family. In 1981, seven months before he died at age 92, he transferred his library and unsurpassed collection of beloved tips to the National Museum of Natural History in Washington, D.C.

The son of a Polish immigrant father and an American mother, Alexander was born in 1889 in Gloversville, New York, in the Mohawk Valley, and early on he developed a passion for the outdoors and natural history. When only sixteen, he vowed to spend his life studying the Tipulidae after the state entomologist in Albany told him that no one in this country could identify the specimens that he had collected.

Alexander went to Cornell, which then had the most distinguished entomological faculty in the United States. Though forced to work his way through, he published almost thirty scientific papers while getting his bachelor's degree in only three and a half years. In 1920, Cornell published his Ph.D. thesis, the previously cited two volumes of *The Crane-Flies of New York*.

In 1922, Alexander joined the faculty of Massachusetts Agricultural College in Amherst, which later became the University of Massachusetts, and there he became renowned as an inspiring, enthusiastic teacher. He had the help of his wife Mabel, who, trained as a secretary, became his coworker on crane flies, and they named the laboratory in their home "Crane Fly Haven." Mabel did all the typing, she indexed all the books and papers, she did all the driving that he never learned to do, and she organized and cataloged almost 14,000 specimens so he could locate any one of them in less than a minute, a feat that staggered visitors. A friend of mine, Dr. Durland Fish, a medical entomologist and now a professor at the Yale University School of Medicine, once had dinner at the Alexanders, and C. P., as he was known, opened the door to a room that was crammed with boxes of unidentified specimens from all over the world. "Another lifetime is needed," he said with a sigh.

As Mass Aggie pupated into UMass, Alexander became head of his department and then dean of the school of science. He found the administrative work demanding, and at the end of each spring term he and Mabel sought to escape across the continent on a collecting trip. After she drove out of Amherst and approached Northampton, he would exclaim, "There, they can't catch me now!"

A variety of materials can be used to tie imitations of crane fly adults. For example, the basic body can be quill shaft inside quill butt, raffia wrapped around the shank, clipped palmered hackle, peacock herl, dubbed fur, and quill stems; legs of bent hog bristle (bent with a heated needle), knotted pheasant or turkey tail fibers (lacquering optional), knotted dark horsehair, knotted black D thread, and knotted skinny dark rubber; wings of grizzly tips, mallard flank feathers, and so on.

The main thing is to make the tied crane fly *big*, an attractive mouthful that will propel fish out of the water, an imitation best represented, to my mind, by the females—female crane flies are larger than the males—of two species of the so-called giant crane flies: *Tipula abdominalis*, found in the eastern half of the United States, and *Holorusia hespera*, found in the West.

Both *abdominalis* and *hespera* are about the same size, with an extended wing span of almost three inches from tip to tip and a body length of almost two inches. The head, thorax, and legs are brown to dark brown while the underside of *abdominalis* is orange and that of *hespera* mostly yellow with some orange. You don't have to get any more particular than that. I've taken trout on gray and brown palmered hackle-bodied crane flies; now, thanks to a quirk of mine, I tie almost all my crane flies with an orange body because the color orange, or a touch of it, seems to appeal to trout. Besides, if it takes a crane fly specialist to tell the difference between *abdominalis* and *hespera*, what would a fish know, other than the dapped imitation whizzing around and landing here and there is a very familiar form that's great to eat.

MATERIALS

Thread:	Danville waxed Flymaster orange, 6/0
Hook:	Streamer hook
Body:	Butt end from Canada goose wing feather or pheasant tail feather; or solid quill shaft from either one of those feathers; or stripped quill sheathing from peacock tail feather; all dyed reddish orange or colored with a permanent marker
Thorax:	Thin cork sheeting
Dapping eye:	Half of Mustad Aberdeen jig hook with upright eye
Ribbing:	Danville waxed Flymaster black, 6/0, optional
Legs:	Six dark brown hog bristles bent to shape with a heated needle; or six turkey tail fibers knotted twice; many patterns call for pheasant tail fibers, but I find them too delicate and too short to knot easily
Wings:	Two grizzly feathers trimmed to shape and tied spent

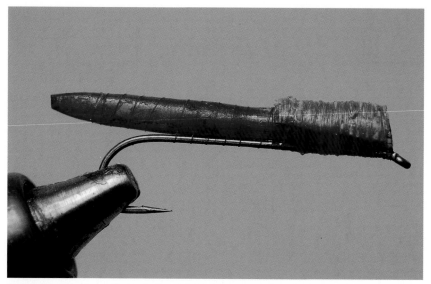

Step 1. This crane fly is similar to but simpler than K's Butt Flying Golden Stone. Place the hook in the vise, tie on a butt body and cork thorax, Krazy Glue in place, and let dry.

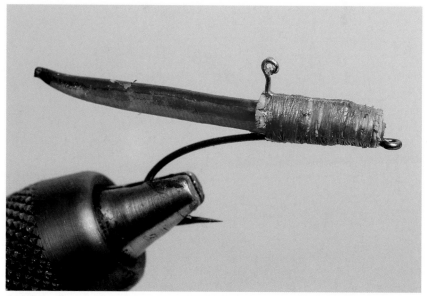

Step 2. Tie the Mustad eye upright on the thorax, and secure with Krazy Glue.

Step 3. Tie on six legs of bent hog bristle, starting with the rear pair, followed by grizzly wings. Tie off, glue the legs in place, let dry, and go dapping with the butt crane fly.

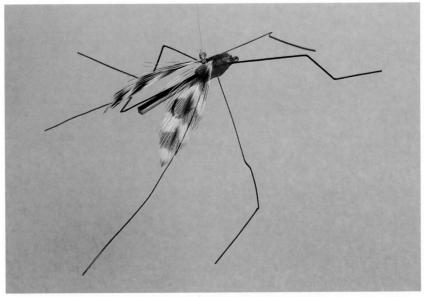

Do the same to tie a solid-quill-shaft crane fly.

This is what the trout sees of an orange-yellow butt crane fly with segmented abdomen and knotted, lacquered turkey-tail fiber legs.

A clipped gray palmered-hackle crane fly with knotted, lacquered turkey-tail fiber legs and wound hackle (the last material to be tied) between the wings—a pattern I sometimes tie and fish because it's light and fluffy enough to catch a puff of wind and gives the appearance of quivering motion.

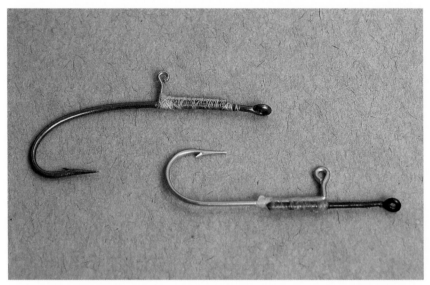

For a hackle-palmered crane fly with an upright eye, tie down the eyed half of a jig hook on top of another hook (as above), or for a combined upright eye and an upright hook, cut off the front half of a streamer hook and tie it to a jig hook. Always secure attachments with Krazy Glue.

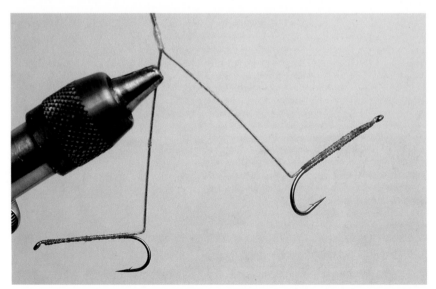

You can tie a pair of crane flies with nylon-coated wire, such as Nylostrand, which is used for tandem streamers.

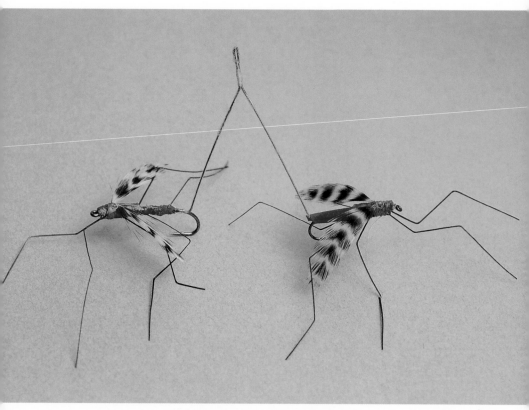

Here they are, ready to go dapping.

You can even create a mating swarm of crane flies (or mayflies)—but make sure it's legal where you fish.

Finally, although I have never tied Jon's Basic British Crane Fly, here are his materials:

MATERIALS

Hook:	Long-shank, 10, 12, or 14
Thread:	Brown
Body:	Brown, pale green, or olive raffia
Ribbing:	Black silk or nylon thread
Legs:	Six knotted pheasant tail fibers
Wings:	Tips of brown cock hackle
Hackle:	Brown, same color as wings

CHAPTER EIGHT

Jumping Grass Shrimp

VERY FEW FRESHWATER FLY FISHERS ARE AWARE OF GRASS SHRIMP and that imitations of them can catch a wide variety of fresh- as well as saltwater fishes. The five major species in the United States belong to the genus *Palaemonetes*, named after Palaemon, the mythological Greek god of ports and harbors. Three of them live in brackish or salt water on the Atlantic and Gulf coasts, but two freshwater species of grass shrimp live in many lakes and slow-moving streams and rivers in parts of the contiguous forty-eight states. On the West Coast, a sixth species of grass shrimp, *Hippolyte clarki*, ranges from Prince William Sound, Alaska, down to Santa Catalina Island, California.

By shrimp I do not mean what most freshwater fly fishers call those curly, quarter-inch shellbacks with tiny flat black dots for eyes, laterally compressed bodies, and four pairs of legs directed forward, plus three pairs directed backward and upward. Also commonly known as scuds, they are actually amphipods. In contrast, true shrimp have prominent, movable stalked eyes and ten legs, which puts them in the suborder Decapoda, Latin for "ten legs." In body form, grass shrimp resemble the shrimp in a shrimp cocktail; except for their dark eyes they are almost completely transparent and are rarely more

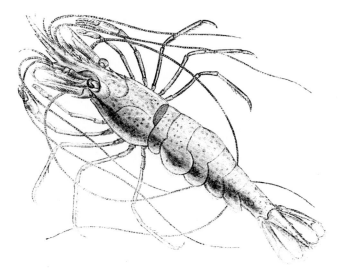

Palaemon serratus *from* A History of the British Stalk-Eyed Crustacea *by Thomas Bell (London: Van Voorst, 1853)*

than two inches long, not counting their antennae. They live for a year, two years at most, with the pregnant females, said to be "in berry," bearing the cluster of fertilized eggs adhered to their underside. Grass shrimp live up to their name by living in submerged vegetation, and given their near transparency, they are also known as glass shrimp and ghost shrimp.

Ecologically, grass shrimp are of immense value. They have an omnivorous appetite that includes the algae and fungi that coat submerged plants, plant detritus, nematodes, polychaete worms, and a host of other creatures, dead and alive. Even that wrecker of marshes and rivers, the United States Army Corps of Engineers, admitted in a 1985 study of grass shrimp that "their ecological importance is unquestioned. Grass shrimp have been extensively documented as prey of fishes and other carnivores and they are instrumental also in transporting energy and nutrients between various . . . trophic levels: primary producers, decomposers, carnivores and detritivores."

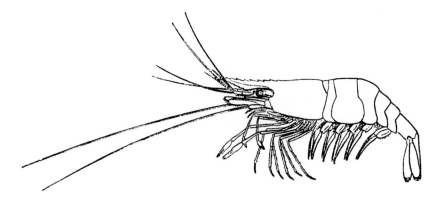

Palaemonetes vulgaris *from Frederick C. Paulmier, "Higher Crustacea of New York City," Bulletin 91, Zoology 12, New York State Museum (Albany: 1905)*

In the seventeenth century, *Palaemon serratus*, a kindred species from British waters that reaches a length of four inches and is known as the common prawn, was one of the animals that Sir William Harvey used to discover the circulation of blood.

Grass shrimp also serve as valuable test animals in bioassays measuring the sublethal and lethal effects of pesticides, heavy metals, petroleum hydrocarbons, and other contaminants. Much research has also been done on their endocrine system because they are quickly able to assume a color that matches their environment. *Palaemonetes vulgaris*, a saltwater species, has, according to Austin B. Williams of the National Museum of Natural History in Washington, "four kinds of pigment under independent hormonal control—red, yellow, white and blue. These pigments are mediated through the eyes by the background on which the animal is found. The source of the hormones is principally the sinus gland complex in the eyestalk and the central nervous system."

Besides their ability to camouflage themselves, grass shrimp can flee from a predator by rapidly flexing their tails. This enables them to dart backward through the water column or jump from the water and skip along the surface, an action that accounts for two more nicknames: jumpers and popcorn shrimp. Apparently they use their antennae, and possibly other body receptors, to sense vibrations in the water caused by the movements of an approaching predator, and to quote from volume II of *The Physiology of Crustacea*, edited by Talbot H. Waterman, "Vibrational stimuli in general evoke only flight reactions or reflex-like jumps directed away from the source of vibration." For fourteen years, I kept a series of brown trout, largemouth and smallmouth bass, juvenile striped bass, white perch, snapper blues, and jack crevalles in a 120-gallon aquarium, and they all loved to eat grass shrimp. Whenever I tossed in a couple dozen shrimp, they'd try to escape from the fish by jumping backward, and on occasion, some attempted to escape by jumping out of the water, only to end up stuck and fried on the inside of the aquarium cover next to the hot lights. It's the jumping behavior that makes grass shrimp imitations ideal for dapping.

Except for Florida bait fishermen, few anglers seem aware of the two freshwater species, *Palaemonetes paludosus* and *kadiakensis*. Many aquatic biologists are unaware of their existence, even though these two shrimp can abound by the millions in lakes, ponds, and rivers. Some years ago while interviewing an outstanding authority on aquatic life, I happened to mention these freshwater shrimp. "Oh, yes, scuds," he said. "No, sir," I said. "I mean shrimp, true shrimp, not scuds." He replied, "Never heard of them." When I started telling him about them, he became excited and asked where he could get information.

Unfortunately information is scattered here and there in scientific papers that more often than not deal with a single narrow aspect of their life history and ecology. Even when standard major references, such as Robert W. Pennak's *Fresh-Water Invertebrates of the United States* and Patrick McCafferty's *Aquatic Entomology*, both first-rate works, cite them, the shrimp receive shriveled notice. But fishermen who stumble across them in nature and use them as bait are blown away by the results.

Take the experience of Dr. John Waldman, until recently the biologist at the Hudson River Foundation for Science and Environmental Research in New York City and now a professor at Queens College in the city. A passionate angler, John related an experience that he had one spring when he visited his in-laws in Florida near Fort Lauderdale. For the previous ten years he had fished the freshwater canal near their home with minnows and worms, and he never did well at all. However, during the spring in question, he happened, for a reason he can't recall, to dip a small mesh net into the canal. To his amazement, the net came up loaded with shrimp that looked exactly like the grass shrimp that he netted back home on the south shore of Long Island to use as bait for white perch. Until that epiphany, he had no idea that such an animal existed in fresh water. He put a couple of the shrimp on his hook, and he began catching fish after fish.

"It wasn't just the fact that these shrimp exist," he exulted, "but that they were so numerous, and that they were the best natural bait I could use. I'd been fishing that spot for ten years and caught very little, but when I cast shrimp in the water they were attacked right away by bass and sunfish. Obviously they loved the shrimp more than the other natural baits."

The freshwater species that he used was *Palaemonetes paludosus*, which gets its specific name from the Latin for marshy or swamp dwelling. *Paludosus* is native to lakes and streams east of the Allegheny Mountains from New Jersey to Florida, and following widespread stocking around 1900, it also found its way into lakes and rivers in Mississippi, Louisiana, Oklahoma, and Texas. On occasion, it has also been reported in brackish water.

The natural abundance of this shrimp can be staggering. In the early 1970s, J. Thomas Beck and Bruce C. Cowell of the University of South Florida found that the population densities in submerged vegetation in the lower Hillsborough River seasonally went from a low of 1.7 million shrimp up to 6.7 million per hectare (a hectare is 2.47

acres). Put another way, the maximum standing crop weighed in at 1,082 pounds per hectare, or about one ton of shrimp per five acres.

Despite this, *paludosus* has remained a greatly ignored natural resource. In a prescient paper delivered way back in 1904 at the Fourth International Fishery Congress in Washington, D.C., S. G. Worth, the superintendent of the United States Fisheries Station in Edenton, North Carolina, extolled the merits of this species (which then had the specific scientific name of *exelipes*) as "a natural food of abundance and cheapness, a food that can be grown out of the natural productiveness of the water, a food corresponding to the natural grass on which wild animals feed, to the nectar of the wild flowers which honey bees gather, conserve and consume. In the fresh-water shrimp we have an example of such a gatherer and conservator . . . a miniature of the salt-water shrimp and prawn. It is meaty, like those species and the American lobster. In fact, in a time of stress it would sustain man. It is a favorite bait for black bass and crappie, two abundant game fishes of the region, the crappie taking this bait when all others are refused.

"The exceeding abundance of fresh-water shrimp," Worth continued, "may be compared with that of house flies in summer, flying ants on their emergence from the decaying stump, or angleworms in favorable soil. They dwell in masses of water mosses and grasses, and in the region referred to such growth is practically universal on all bottom. Hundreds of acres of water in many counties are teeming with this unrivalled natural food of fish. It exists by the millions and by the ton. From the foregoing it is practically certain that this species is adapted to broadcast distribution in the temperate zone of the globe, and capable of becoming a resource of incalculable value."

In 1972 I happened to be in Los Angeles to cover a track meet for *Sports Illustrated*. To pass the time in my hotel room, I was tying grass shrimp imitations when George Long, assigned to photograph the meet for the magazine, knocked on the door. I opened it, and George, a fly fisherman, went gaga at my imitations.

"Could I have one?" he asked.

"Take one," I said. He did, and off we went to the meet.

A year later out of the blue, George wrote, "I was on a fishing story on the Colorado River below the Hoover Dam. We were photographing Virgil Ward, who has a TV fishing show. They used everything—Bombers, Flatfish, spinners, poppers and cheese—nothing would work. They were talking about fish feeding on freshwater shrimp. I told them about your shrimp. Virgil tried the one I had and caught a couple of 2½-pound to 3-pound rainbows—before a rock caught the shrimp. It worked so well, I hoped we could get a few more from you."

When I read this I thought that the rainbows had taken the shrimp imitations simply because they looked tasty or perhaps they had some distant evolutionary memory of shrimp. After all, smallmouth bass in the Croton Reservoir, near where I then lived, took the imitation despite the absence of shrimp, although perhaps they took it for a shedder crayfish. Years later, however, I learned that rainbow trout in the lower Colorado had to be aware of *paludosus*. In 1950, the California Department of Fish and Game had stocked that part of the Colorado after importing them from Florida.

The other freshwater grass shrimp is *Palaemonetes kadiakensis*, and its specific name remains a mystery. *Kadiakensis* would indicate that it was discovered in Kodiak, Alaska, and named by a taxonomist who had trouble spelling. In fact, *kadiakensis* was not discovered in Kodiak, and no one knows why or how it got its mangled name. *Kadiakensis* is not found within more than a thousand miles of Kodiak; instead it ranges from southern Ontario all the way down to northeastern Mexico. Despite the mystery, the name continues to stand under the rules of the International Commission on Zoological Nomenclature, which determines the validity of names for neozoological and paleozoological species.

In the past, *kadiakensis* was reported in all the Great Lakes, although "nowhere very abundant" in Lake Ontario, to quote from

A Biological Survey of the Lake Ontario Watershed, published in 1939 by the New York State Conservation Department. Other sources report that the species is numerous in the Mississippi River and its watershed tributaries and lakes in Ohio, Kentucky, Tennessee, Indiana, Illinois, Wisconsin, Minnesota, Iowa, Missouri, Oklahoma, Arkansas, Mississippi, and Louisiana. And that's not all. *Kadiakensis* also occurs in Texas, Alabama, Georgia, and northern Florida, and in 1988 it was even reported in Vermont, in all likelihood the result of stocking.

In a two-volume study of Lake Maxinkuckee, Indiana, published in 1920, Barton W. Evermann and Howard W. Clark noted that while *kadiakensis* was "not common in or about the lake . . . immense numbers of this shrimp were found [in the Little River] in masses of Ceratophyllum from which the transparent creatures jumped with great alacrity when hauled out of the water." As with *paludosus*, its numbers can be enormous. A 1970s study of Missouri ponds found that summer populations ranged from 700,000 to 3.4 million per hectare.

Three other *Palaemonetes* species—*vulgaris, intermedius,* and *pugio*—are found on the Atlantic and Gulf coasts, generally depending upon the salinity of the water. As a rule of thumb, *pugio* occurs in the least brackish water, *intermedius* in more brackish water, and *vulgaris* in even more brackish water.

These three coastal species look so much like one another, as well as their two freshwater cousins, that a magnifying glass is needed to tell the five of them apart. In fact, no one would even know there are three coastal species were it not for Lipke B. Holthuis, a Dutch specialist whose massive two-volume study, *A General Revision of the Palaemonidae (Crustacea Decapoda Natantia) of the Americas*, was published by the Allan Hancock Foundation at the University of Southern California in 1951 and 1952.

In the 1960s I was unaware of this definitive work when I happened upon hordes of grass shrimp in the tidal Hudson River and the tributary Croton River while doing field research for a book, *The*

Hudson River, A Natural and Unnatural History. In my book I referred to the species as *Palaemonetes vulgaris* because that was the scientific name used in all New York State references.

After my book came out, I followed up my interest in grass shrimp—they are intriguing animals—and in so doing ran across a reference to Holthuis's work. I ordered it immediately from the Allan Hancock Foundation, and it arrived just as I was about to fly to Kansas City to do a piece for *Sports Illustrated* on Otis Taylor, the Chiefs' star wide receiver. I took the two volumes with me to read on the plane, and somewhere high over Indiana or Illinois, I read in volume two that Holthuis had discovered that there was not just one coastal species named *Palaemonetes vulgaris*, but two other species as well. Not only had the two never before been described or named, but they had been pickled and preserved as *Palaemonetes vulgaris* in every relevant laboratory, university, and museum collection that he examined.

Holthuis separated the three species based largely on the differences between their rostrums—the name for the beak or nose that extends forward from between the eyes as shown on pages 89 and 90. He named the two new species *pugio* and *intermedius*, *pugio* from the Latin for "dagger" because the point of its rostrum is smooth like a dagger, and *intermedius* because the number of serrations, notches, or teeth on its rostrum is intermediate between those on the rostrums of *pugio* and *vulgaris*. To top it off, Holthuis condemned all the ecological references to *vulgaris* as invalid because they could actually be about the two species he had discovered.

At once I realized that not only was I probably wrong in automatically naming grass shrimp I had collected *vulgaris*, but loads of scientists in the country who had also been using *vulgaris* as their lab animal might have been using the wrong animal, and that could, possibly, invalidate years of test results.

Back home, I used a magnifying glass to examine the grass shrimp I had preserved from the Hudson and Croton rivers, and, lo, all were *pugio*, not one *vulgaris*. I phoned a good acquaintance who worked with *vulgaris* to tell him that his shrimp were undoubtedly *pugio*, based on Holthuis's study published almost twenty years before. Instead of thanking me for alerting him, he exclaimed, "You're full of it! What the hell would you know?" and hung up. Later I read that he said that he was involved with *pugio*, with nary a word or hint about *vulgaris*. Thus does science march on.

If you want to know which species of *Palaemonetes* you have, be they from fresh, brackish, or salt water, look at the differences that Holthuis discerned. However, note that I do not tie a rostrum in my

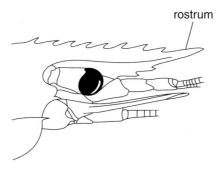

P. pugio. *Rostrum tip smooth and pointed like a dagger. Brackish to almost fresh water on Atlantic and Gulf coasts. (Illustrations on pages 89 and 90 adapted from Holthuis, courtesy of the University of Southern California on behalf of the Hancock Foundation Archive.)*

P. intermedius. *Rostrum upper tip toothed at end and lower tip smooth toward end. Brackish to salt water on Atlantic and Gulf coasts.*

posterior orbital margin

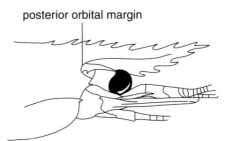

P. vulgaris. *The first two teeth on upper rostrum behind the posterior orbital margin on the carapace. Brackish to salt water on Atlantic and Gulf coasts.*

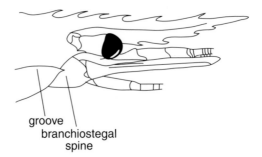

groove
branchiostegal
spine

P. paludosus. *Rostrum slender reaching to or beyond scaphocerite; upper rostrum margin somewhat concave. Branchiostegal spine just below branchiostegal groove. Fresh water: east of Alleghenies, New Jersey to Florida; also Louisiana, Texas, Oklahoma, and probably Missouri.*

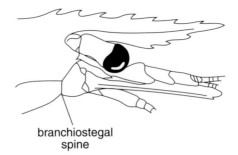

branchiostegal
spine

P. kadiakensis. *Rostrum upper margin somewhat convex. Branchiostegal spine distinct distance below branchiostegal groove. Fresh water: central United States and southern Canada, southern United States, northeastern Mexico.*

patterns because it would interfere with tying the leader, and besides, as the fish have taught me, a rostrum is not necessary. After all, a rostrum is transparent.

Inasmuch as I believe in tying from living creatures, I have, from time to time, kept *pugio* in a five-gallon aquarium atop my desk and fed them tidbits of chopped earthworms, canned cat food, and, occasionally, smoked salmon, which causes their stomachs, up near their heads, to turn orange. Predators themselves, they will pounce on any moulting brother or sister whose soft, unprotected body swiftly becomes a corpus delecti, and if I stock forty of fifty in the aquarium, over time, even when I feed them, I eventually wind up with just two shrimp, each cautiously eyeing the other because the one who moults first is going to end up as the last supper.

I have two different patterns for grass shrimp. The first pattern, relatively new and easier to keep near or on the surface for dapping or casting, has a quill butt body; the second pattern has a clear wrapped body.

MATERIALS FOR THE QUILL-BODIED GRASS SHRIMP

Hook:	6, 8, or 10 straight-eye streamer hook
Thread:	Danville waxed Flymaster white, 6/0, and Danville monofilament fine
Eyes:	Two shirt pins (blackened heads) or burnt mono
Small antennae:	Polar bear hair, or white hen hackle whisks
Long antennae:	Two hog bristles, or stripped white hackle stems
Underbody:	White wool
Body:	Butt end of Canada goose wing feather

MATERIALS FOR THE
QUILL-BODIED GRASS SHRIMP
CONTINUED

Legs: Polar bear hair, or white hen hackle
                         whisks in a bunch or on one side of a
                         hackle stem, or hog bristles crimped to
                         shape with a heated needle

Tail (optional):   White hen hackle feather trimmed
                         to shape

Plus Krazy Glue and Sally Hansen's Hard as Nails polish

Step 1. Given that shrimp flee predators by going backward, place the eye of the hook in the vise, tie on the short antennae projecting past the bend of the hook, followed by the long antennae, and secure with polish. Grass shrimp have two long antennae, one on each side, but sometimes I tie two on each side to give the fly more movement because the antennae undulate on the retrieve.

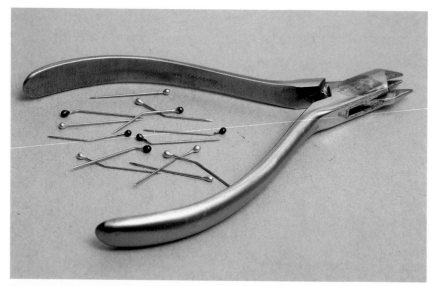

Step 2. With dental pliers, bend two shirt pins at equal angles, and blacken pin heads with Pantone marker.

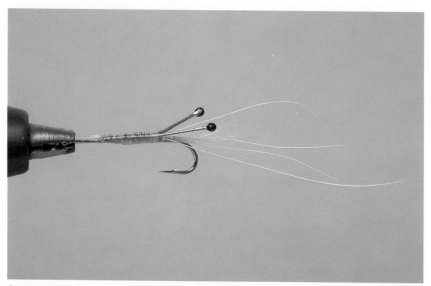

Step 3. Tie in a pin on each side of the shank so that the stalked eyes stand out, secure them with Krazy Glue, and let dry.

Step 4. Tie in white wool to serve as the tapered underbody.

Step 5. Tie off the tapered underbody with overhand knots, and cut the thread.

Step 6. Cut butts at the angle shown, and clean them of pith.

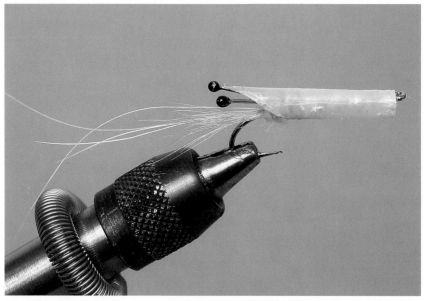

Step 7. Select a butt for fit by sliding it toward the eyes over the wool; if the butt fits snugly, remove it, add a drop of Krazy Glue to the head of the wool, and slide the butt back over the wool so that the inside of the butt sticks to the Krazy Glue.

Step 8. With fine monofilament tying thread, tie in a strip of white hen hackle in reverse position to serve as legs and swimmerets; they should move when the fly is retrieved.

Step 9. To put on the optional legs, place the shrimp upside down in the vise. Use monofilament thread to tie on five hog bristles equally bent in a V, one after the other slanting forward. Tie them off, secure with Krazy Glue, and let dry. Light a candle, and heat a needle in the flame. Very, very carefully and with the lightest touch, use the heated needle to put realistic bends in each of the ten legs. If the needle is too hot or your touch clumsy, you will amputate the leg, and it is a pain to tie in a replacement. So again, be very, very careful. The heated legs will retain their bends permanently when fished. These legs do not necessarily make any difference to the fish so far as I know, but they do make fanatics like you and me very happy with ourselves.

Step 10. For the optional tail, insert the stem of a feather shaped like the tail of a shrimp in the rear of the butt, and secure it in place by holding the shrimp head down and gingerly adding a drop of Krazy Glue inside the butt.

THE CLEAR WRAPPED-BODY GRASS SHRIMP

I use two different hook types for this pattern. The original pattern I started tying almost forty years ago uses Mustad bronze hook 37160 with a turned-up eye and a curved shank that matches the curve of a shrimp and its backward retreat when in flight. The saltwater version is tied on Mustad stainless-steel hook 37160S.

The second hook for this pattern can be any streamer hook, with a turned-down eye, that matches the length of the size of the shrimp you want to imitate. Using dental pliers, I bend the shank of the hook so that the bend and barb ride upright and the bend marks the line between the abdomen and the thorax. Do not even think of using a straight-eye streamer hook, because that would make it very difficult to get a leader through the eye of the hook (the antennae, short and long, would block it).

I first tied this pattern on the curved hook for striped bass in the lower Croton River, and over the years it has gone on to take steelhead, rainbow, brown, brook, and cutthroat trout; Atlantic salmon in Canada, Iceland, Scotland, and Norway; coho and chinook salmon in Washington state and Alaska; smallmouth and largemouth bass; yellow perch; black crappies, bluegills, and pumpkinseeds; white perch; Atlantic mackerel; bluefish; and bonefish in the Bahamas and Mexico. When cast, not dapped, a size 6 to 10 bent streamer hook does well for bonefish because it does not alarm them with a splash. Remember, however, that a bronzed hook fished in salt water should be rinsed in fresh water after use.

MATERIALS

Hook:	Streamer, TDE, size 2 to 8, bent with dental pliers
Thread:	Danville monofilament fine and Danville waxed Flymaster orange, 6/0
Body:	Ten- to twelve-inch-long strip of Clor-Pane, sliced $1/16$ inch wide with a double cutter obtainable at an art supply store; Clor-Pane is the trade name for transparent plastic sheeting used to cover office equipment and furniture
Eyes:	Burnt 50-pound mono
Long antennae:	Two hog bristles, or stripped white hackle feather stems, or fine mono line
Short antennae:	Polar bear hair, or hog bristle, or white hen hackle, or finer mono line
Tail (optional):	Clor-Pane trimmed to triangular shape
Legs:	Polar bear hair, white hen hackle fibers, fine mono, or the previously described five pairs of hog bristles tied bent to shape with a heated needle

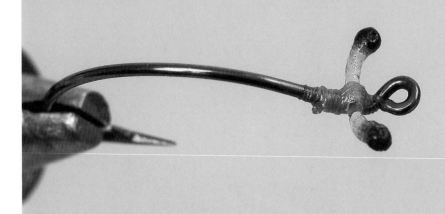

Step 1. With orange thread, tie down the burnt mono eyes with figure-eights on top of the shank next to the hook eye. Tie off, remove the thread, secure the eyes with Krazy Glue, and let dry. I use orange thread because it gives a spark of life, or so I like to believe. If desired, you can wind the thread down the shank, or wrap the shank with silver Mylar, or whatever material you fancy, so that it shows through the finished fly—I have even tied shrimp so that they showed, so I thought, their internal organs. Remember, this pattern is transparent, so you can play with it all you wish to give it that added dimension that satisfies your fly-tying soul.

Step 2. After turning the hook bottom up in the vise and tying the short and long antennae below the eyes as previously described, use the double cutter to slice a $1/16$-inch-wide, 10- to 12-inch-long strip of transparent Clor-Pane (colored red here so that you can see it).

Step 3. Tie in an end of the Clor-Pane with the monofilament thread, and start wrapping a tapered body around the shank.

Step 4. Upon finishing the tapered body, you can add whatever kind of legs you want. Then tie off, apply nail polish, let dry, enclose the bend of the hook in forceps, and coat the whole body with five-minute epoxy, taking care to rotate the shrimp to coat evenly and prevent the epoxy from touching the legs or antennae.

VARIATIONS OF THE PATTERN

To tie a pink shrimp or one of any color, all natural materials are best dyed, but use a permanent marking pen on the Clor-Pane.

A speckled shrimp has long antennae of grizzly hackle stems, short antennae and legs of mallard flank feather fibers, and a laid-down back of a mallard flank feather coated with five-minute epoxy.

Transparent Clor-Pane gives the tier room to do interior decorating with innards.

A trio of red shrimp with quill bodies and claws of shaped spade hackle on double salmon hooks look like cooked lobsters. Tied in olive green they become crayfish.

CHAPTER NINE

Quill Minnows, Credit-Card Minnows, and the Kat's Meow

I N THE 1938 EDITION OF *MAKING AND USING THE FLY AND LEADER*, Paul Young, the Michigan rod maker whose midge rod and Strawman nymph made him a cult figure, included a sketch of his Quill Minnow.

Young wrote that, tied on a long-shank size 6 to 8 hook, it was "a very successful surface or near-surface fly . . . extremely light and cast nicely.

"I have had several of these quill minnow taken and kept by monster browns, in broad daylight, when no amount of dry fly casting would raise them. . . . I make some three inches long, which are used on baby tarpon and other sea fish which run into brackish water."

Young was an accomplished tier, but unless you're bent on following the complicated directions for his Quill Minnow, which, among a number of things, called for the hook to be inserted inside the butt and heating a wire to melt paraffin to seal the opening, all you need to do is tie the butt to the top of the shank of the hook, plug the front open end with a piece of solid quill shaft or cork, and secure it in place with Krazy Glue, unknown in Young's day.

Paul Young's Quill Minnow took monster browns when dry flies failed.

Adding eyes helps. In my experience, the eyes have it. Except for the snapper blues that almost always attacked the tail end of the bait-fish—shiners, killies, sawbellies—that I fed the inhabitants of my 120-gallon aquarium, all focused on the eyes of the prey and engulfed them head first. Hard-shell crayfish were another story. If a crayfish was taken head first, it would wield its claws like a dentist gone wild, causing the fish to spit it out, bat it around, and then inhale it tail first. Even a 7-pound smallmouth, the biggest fish I ever had in the tank, did this for the year that I kept him before returning him to the Croton Reservoir. He lived for crayfish but never ate any of the black-nosed dace that I put in to round out his diet. Instead he let the dace serve as his personal grooms, holding still and even yawning while they nibbled away at bits of loose skin around his mouth.

If you wish, skip the butt and instead use a solid quill shaft as the basic body for a minnow imitation. Both butt and shaft make ideal dapping or fly-rod plugs.

MATERIALS

Hook:	Size 2 to 10 streamer hooks
Thread:	Danville fine transparent
Body:	Quill butt (or solid quill shaft)
Cover:	Silver Mylar sleeve
Eyes:	Dowled yellow and black eyes, or pasted eyes

Besides eyes and silver Mylar, you can cover the butt or shaft with whatever you want, from hen hackle to permanent markers and India ink.

The variations are limitless.

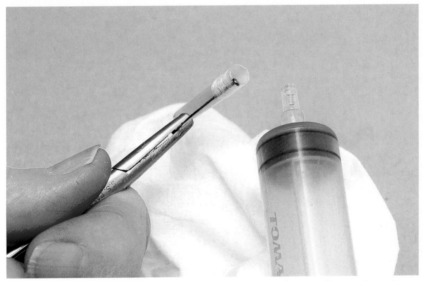

You can also add to the inside of a butt by inserting a rattle capsule or a drop of olive oil to create a moving globule.

CREDIT-CARD MINNOWS

I call this tying with trash, and the trash I most love are expired credit cards because they make a form imitating a minnow that's badly wounded, just the way most people feel when the credit-card bill arrives in the mail. I use scissors to cut the shape of a minnow or a baitfish. You can also cut up a cereal box or shirt cardboard, but do not make the form too big; cardboard is on the soft side, and pressure from the tying thread is likely to bend it out of shape. (Don't worry about the cardboard getting wet when fished because the finished minnow will be waterproofed with a skin and covered with five-minute epoxy.) You can also use shears to cut a form from aluminum cans—sardine cans are particularly fitting—but take care that the sharp edges do not cut the tying thread. You can avoid this by tying gently with a thicker thread.

MATERIALS

Hook:	Streamer hook of your choice
Basic body:	Any plastic credit card, cardboard, aluminum cans, or any other suitable trash
Inner tying thread:	Any color to tie the minnow form, which will be covered later by kitchen foil, silver Mylar, or other outer body material of your artistic angling choice
Tail:	Fluffy hen hackle fibers, marabou, or whatever, again your choice
Body cement:	Krazy Glue
Outer body or skin:	Aluminum foil, silver Mylar, or pearlescent Mylar, yet again your choice
Outer tying thread:	Danville monofilament fine
Eyes:	Stick-on or painted

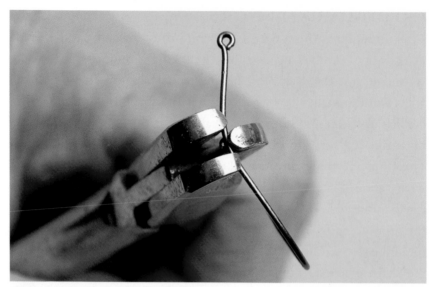

Step 1. With dental pliers, bend the hook shank to the right or left in imitation of the curved-to-the-side backbone of a wounded or crippled minnow that's wallowing and flip-flopping on the surface.

Step 2. Cut the credit card in the form of a minnow that matches the length of the hook shank. Insert the hook in the vise, tie on the form, glue it in place, and let dry.

Step 3. Tie in the tail, cut foil to shape, and fold it over both sides of the form. Tie it down with mono thread, secure it with Krazy Glue, let dry, and add eyes. These are finished minnows.

THE KAT'S MEOW

Upright eyes are on the left, split-shot eyes on the right—these Kat's Meows are lethal either cast or as a dropper for a dapper.

The Kat's Meow is a $\frac{1}{64}$-ounce fly-rod jig on size 10 to 14 hooks. I first tied it back in the late 1960s by pressing split-shot on the head of a hook and adding a tail of hackle fibers and two fine strands of silver Mylar. I used it to catch alewives coming in from the Atlantic to spawn in the lower Croton River. Later I named it the Kat's Meow after Dmitri "Mitya" Kotyik, one of my wife's two Siamese cats, and it has gone on to catch around a hundred species of fish, some more than five pounds despite the jig's diminutive size. It's like offering the last piece of fudge to a fat person. Use it as a dropper when dapping.

A nymph, in this case Pteronarcys californica, *can also be used as a dapping dropper.*

CHAPTER TEN

Hewitt's Skaters

It is curious that some of the most deadly flies of the past have become almost extinct.

——Richard Salmon, *Trout Flies* (1975)

"Will you walk into my parlor?" said the Spider to the Fly;
"'Tis the prettiest little parlor that ever did you spy."

——Mary Howitt, *The Spider and the Fly* (1844)

RICHARD SALMON'S STATEMENT CERTAINLY APPLIES TO THE Neversink Skater devised by Edward R. Hewitt in the 1930s, as well as to misnamed spiders, misnamed and confusing because, unlike natural spiders, artificial spiders have a tail while skaters do not. To make matters possibly more confusing, according to Hewitt's account in *A Trout and Salmon Fisherman for Seventy-five Years*, he modeled his skater that looks like a spider on butterflies. Why? He saw large trout leaping for butterflies as they dipped and danced across the Neversink River in the Catskills where he had his camp. The butterflies sometimes touched the water, but they always kept moving, and to imitate their delicate fluttering up-and-down flight, he used the stiffest, longest hackles he had on a size 16 light Model Perfect hook, "the lightest hook that I know that will hold a big trout." The resulting Neversink Skater had the diameter of a silver dollar, about two inches, and the sparsely tied hackle offered little air resistance when cast. For the same reason, the fly had no wings, and it had no tail to inhibit movement on the water.

The fly proved to be extraordinarily effective in this country, yet when Hewitt tied on a cream-colored Neversink Skater when he went to fish Loch Ordie in Scotland, his ghillie looked at it and scornfully said, "Ye will catch no fush with yon feather duster."

Hewitt had barely begun casting when a great trout leapt high in the air with the Neversink Skater in its mouth. The $4^{1}/_{2}$-pounder was soon in the boat, but the ghillie harrumphed, "That wur an accident." Hewitt went on to take a dozen trout from 4 to $5^{1}/_{2}$ pounds. He noted, "These large fish were coming up so fast from deep water that they could not stop at the surface, but went high in the air when they reached the fly."

Like the skater, the spider proved successful, but both flies have long been out of mind and out of fashion despite A. J. McClane's declaration in *The Practical Fly Fisherman* (1953): "Of all trout flies, the one you can least afford to be without is the spider."

One reason why the skater and the spider are all but unknown today is because stiff long hackles went the way of the dodo when the fly-fishing world swung wildly in the direction of teensy-weensy genetic hackle for teensy-weensy flies.

Fortunately, there is a solution: Coq de Leon spade feathers from Leon in northern Spain, where conditions are said to be just right for producing such strong, lustrous, and gorgeous feathers, unmatched by any others I have ever seen. Coq de Leon feathers come in two basic types: Pardo feathers that are speckled and Indio feathers that are not, and both types come in a variety of colors. I buy mine from a member of the breeders association in Leon, Jose Manuel Cenador Cela, who also ties flies, teaches fly tying, and guides. (Jose's email address is josema777@gmail.com.)

Pardo feathers on the left, Indio on the right

I tie the skaters on Tiemco 102Y size 17 hooks. The tying is very easily done with two feathers, but as Eric Leiser told me some years ago, there are two simple tricks in tying the skater: The first is to tie the feathers dull side to dull side, and the second is to push the two feathers together as much as possible with your thumbs. Do this and the skaters will stand right up on the tying table.

Three Pardo skaters and an Indio skater

A Pardo skater close up

A front and side view of an Indio skater

Howard Bartholomew, a good friend of the late Art Flick, ties these slightly longer and bushier Flick patterns to dap for trout and smallmouth bass. The longer than usual hackle on two of the four came from fifteen-year-old Metz necks that Howard fortunately set aside before hackles started shrinking.

Gray Fox Variant (Ephemera guttulata): *Partridge Captain Hamilton hook, size 10; ginger tail; Rhode Island red quill body; ginger, grizzly, and red hackle*

Cream Variant (Potamanthus distinctus): *Partridge Captain Hamilton hook, size 10; ginger tail; Rhode Island red quill; and ginger hackle*

Dun Variant (Isonychia bicolor): *Herter's Gaelic Supreme hook, size 12; dun tail; Rhode Island red quill body; and dun hackle*

Indio Dun (Isonychia bicolor): *Herter's Gaelic Supreme hook, size 10; dun tail; dun quill body; and dun hackle from an Indio spade feather*

CHAPTER ELEVEN

Irish and Scottish Dapping Flies

NICK RAE OF NORTH LANARKSHIRE, SCOTLAND, TIED THE DOZEN dapping flies shown here. Now 31, he began fishing as a boy, and after studying fisheries and fish farming at college in Dumfries, he worked for three years at a sporting estate in the Highlands that had many trout lochs and a beat on the River Spey. For the last nine years he has worked for the Glasgow Angling Centre, the largest retail tackle store in the United Kingdom, where he is the assistant manager of the mail order department. Nick has also fished in Ireland, Norway, Australia, and New Zealand, and at this writing, he is planning a trip to the United States to fish for striped bass.

LOCH ORDIE MATERIALS

Hook:	Low-water salmon single hook, size 6 to 10
Thread:	Black
Body:	Large cock or hen hackles, tied from rear with natural curve of feathers facing forward
Rear hackle:	Black, dark brown, or dark ginger, followed by light brown or light ginger hackle
Head hackle:	White hackle

This Loch Ordie variant has all black hackles and a head of blue hackle.

LOCH ORDIE DADDY LONGLEGS
MATERIALS

Hook:	Small treble, size 12, inserted with leader upon completion of tying
Tube:	Small ½-inch-long plastic tube with large enough bore to slide small treble hook upon after fly is tied
Thread:	Black
Extended body:	1-inch length of fine Larva Lace or Ultra Lace tubing, yellow or olive, tied on top of tube
Legs:	Six knotted golden pheasant tail fibers
Hackle:	Two or three light ginger hackles
Head hackle:	White cock hackle

This is a tube fly, with all materials tied on the tube, tied at the request of one of Nick's customers to improve the hooking qualities of the fly. It can also be tied on a single hook.

CLARET BUMBLE MATERIALS

Hook:	Kamasan B170 or any traditional wet-fly hook, size 6
Thread:	Black
Tail:	No. 11 Glo Brite Yarn
Rib:	Oval gold tinsel
Body:	Claret seal fur
Hackle:	One claret and one large black cock hackle palmered together
Head hackle:	Dyed blue English partridge

This is a slight variation of the excellent Irish pattern, Kingsmill Moore Claret Bumble.

FIERY BROWN BUMBLE
MATERIALS

Hook:	Kamasan B170 or any traditional wet-fly hook, size 6
Thread:	Black
Tail:	No. 4 or 5 Glo Brite Yarn
Rib:	Oval gold tinsel
Body:	Red seal fur
Hackle:	One blood red and one fiery brown large cock hackle palmered together
Head hackle:	Dyed orange guinea fowl

This is a variation of an Irish pattern.

OLIVE DAP MATERIALS

Hook:	Kamasan B179 or any traditional wet-fly hook, size 6
Thread:	Black
Tail:	Golden pheasant tail fibers
Hackle:	Two olive grizzly cock hackles wound from rear with natural curve of the hackles facing forward

BLUE ZULU MATERIALS

Hook: Low-water salmon single hook,
                         size 6 to 10
Thread: Black
Tag: Flat silver tinsel
Body: Black seal fur
Body hackle: Claret and black hackles palmered
                         together
Rib: Oval silver tinsel
Head hackle: Kingfisher blue cock hackle

The original Zulu, still used extensively, is dressed as above but omits the blue hackle head.

BLACK AND PEACOCK
MATERIALS

Hook:	Low-water salmon single hook, size 6 to 10
Thread:	Black
Tag:	Flat gold tinsel
Rib:	Gold oval tinsel
Body:	Peacock herl
Hackle:	Two large black cock hackles

PALMER MATERIALS

Hook:	Low-water salmon single hook, size 6 to 10
Thread:	Black
Rib:	Gold oval tinsel
Body:	Red seal fur
Hackle:	Two large cock furnace or brown hackles palmered
Head hackle:	Cock furnace or brown hackle

Different color combinations are used, but this is the most common pattern.

BLACK PENNELL MATERIALS

Hook:	Low-water salmon single hook, size 6 to 10
Thread:	Black
Tag:	Flat silver tinsel
Tail:	Golden pheasant tippets
Rib:	Oval silver tinsel
Body:	Black floss
Hackle:	Two large black cock hackles

FORE AND AFT MATERIALS

Hook:	Low-water salmon single hook, size 6 to 10
Thread:	Black
Tail:	Black cock hackle fibers
Rear hackle:	One large black cock hackle
Body:	Red floss
Front hackle:	One large black cock hackle

There are many variations of this type of pattern.

EASY DOES IT MATERIALS

Hook: Low-water salmon single hook,
                     size 6 to 10
Body: Flat gold tinsel
Hackle: Two large brown or furnace cock hackles

Again, many variations exist of this type of pattern.

IRISH DAPPING FLIES

Peter Dunne of Durrow, County Laois, Ireland, won so many world fly-tying championships in Norway that he was prohibited from competing again, with his last wins—three gold and two silver medals—coming in 2002. The *Laois Nationalist* headlined news of the ban: "Too Good to Take on the World." Peter, who has fished in England, the United States, Canada, and Australia, also organizes and directs the Irish Open Fly-Tying Championships, which attract both professional and amateur tiers from all over the world. So take that, Norway!

DUNNE'S DAPPING MAYFLIES

DUNNE'S DAPPING CRANE FLIES

BOB MEAD
CONFESSES

ALTHOUGH BOB MEAD OF SCOTIA, NEW YORK, WHO LOVES TO TIE incredibly realistic flies, also loves to fly-fish, he long resisted my appeals that he try dapping with the blowline that I sent him. Almost all the fly fishers to whom I've given blowline have absolutely refused to try dapping for reasons that I can only deem doctrinal, but I found Bob Mead's resistance strange because dapping would allow him to fish his incredibly realistic flies in an incredibly realistic fashion. At long last he did try it, and his emailed confession below expresses the concerns he had to conquer, the fears he had to fight, and the qualms he had to quiet, in order to take this courageous step. Faint-of-heart fly fishers, fear not the fly-reel fascists—follow Bob Mead and go dapping!

11/17/2005 6:46:41 PM Eastern Standard Time

Now you have gone and done it, my friend! Hooked me good and true on a new and fascinating method of fly fishing! Well, new to me at least!

I admit to being a bit skeptical when I first learned a spinning reel was a necessity and, while admitting things, also to a momentary whiff of a thought that perhaps my old friend had inhaled once too many times the fumes of the preservative used to embalm his stonefly nymphs.

However, the more I listened, the more reasonable it sounded, and when a few days later I received a spool of the required floss blowline in my post box, attempt at dapping became inevitable.

I waited till fall to give it a try. Mind you, the lengthy wait was only for the following reasons: the right conditions, the correct breeze, and a good water level. The fact that there would be a scant handful of anglers on the entire length of the river at the time had absolutely nothing to do with it.

Just to be safe, I mean, to be a bit closer to where I wanted to try dapping, I parked my vehicle a couple of hundred yards beyond an empty fishermen's parking area and then quickly pulled on waders and rigged up. My trusty old fly rod seemed to cringe when I pushed the ring slip down over the reel foot. What heresy!

To be certain that nothing snagged on that big spinning reel handle and knob, I kept that end of my rod safely tucked under my vest all the way to the river. Then glancing upstream and down and thinking only of how nice it was to have an entire section of river to myself, I began practicing the basic "Boyle Rules of Dapping."

They were actually quite easily followed. The gentle breeze did most of the work. It lifted the twenty-foot section of floss, 6-pound-test spinning line, and my leader out over the water, causing the fly to realistically dip and dance on and off the surface.

It didn't take long to learn just how much raising and lowering of the rod tip it took to assist the wind so I would occasionally get short floats between bounces. It amazed me too that I had a certain amount of control over the general surface areas I wanted to cover.

The sun had begun to slip behind the mountains, and it was getting outright chilly. I was about to call it quits, being quite satisfied with my effort, when the gods smiled down on me and a small trout came right out of the water to grab my fly!

It surprised me because since my arrival I had not seen a single rise, had not moved from where I entered, and had not expected to do anything but practice technique. I immediately learned why the quick pickup of line via a spinning reel was required. Releasing the 10-inch fish with a smile, I remember saying, "Well, I'll be damned!"

I look forward to doing more dapping come spring. It certainly deserves more than the late afternoon hour I gave it in October. It works!

INDEX